*Translated and edited by*
*Thomas G. Bergin* CORNELL UNIVERSITY

# THE
# PRINCE

BY

*Niccolò Machiavelli*

*Appleton–Century–Crofts, Inc.*
NEW YORK

# Contents

# CONTENTS

# Important Dates in Machiavelli's Life

1469   Born, May 3, in Florence.

1498   Appointed secretary to the Chancery in Soderini's government.

1499   Mission to Caterina Sforza at Forlì.

1500   Mission to France. Meeting with Louis XII and the Cardinal de Rouen.

1502   Marriage to Marietta Corsini. Mission to Romagna and first meeting with Cesare Borgia.

1503   Further contacts with Borgia in Romagna and Rome.

1504   Second mission to France.

1506   With Julius II in Umbria and Emilia.

1508   Mission to the Emperor Maximilian in Bolzano.

1509   Fall of Pisa.

1510   Third mission to France.

1512   Return of the Medici. Machiavelli dismissed. Retirement to San Casciano and beginning of the *Commentary on Livy*.

1513   Imprisonment, torture, and release. Writing of *The Prince*.

1515   Probable date of the composition of *La Mandragola*.

1519   Machiavelli consulted by the Medici on the Florentine Constitution.

1520   *The Art of War, The Life of Castruccio Castracane*. Commissioned to write the *History of Florence*.

1524   Probable date of composition of *Clizia*.

1525   First part of the *History of Florence* finished and dedicated to Clement VII.

1526   Mission to Lombardy on behalf of Clement. Meeting with Guicciardini.

1527   The Medici expelled from Florence. Death of Machiavelli, June 22.

ITALY
AT THE CLOSE OF
THE 15th CENTURY

# Introduction

The attentive reader of *The Prince* will be able to piece together from the work itself an adequate outline of the political scene in which Machiavelli worked, lived, and wrote. Yet for a better understanding of the times out of which *The Prince* emerges a brief summary of events may be useful. A certain precarious balance of power existed in Italy in the 15th century. The country was divided into five important states: the Republic of Venice, the Duchy of Milan, the so-called Republic of Florence, run by the Medici, the Church, and the Kingdom of Naples. Frequent wars between these powers did break out; yet, as Machiavelli indicates, the wiser princes saw the advantages of preserving the equilibrium and, above all, of keeping foreigners out of Italian politics. Unfortunately for Italy, other countries were moving rapidly towards unification, and the peninsular balance of power was not adapted to deal with the new situation. In France the marriage of Anne of Brittany to Charles VIII (1491) enormously increased the strength of the ruling family, while the patient reforms of Louis XI, aimed at uniting the nation under a strong monarch, had begun to bear fruit. Similarly in Spain the union of Castile and Aragon in the marriage of Ferdinand and Isabella (1469), the conquest of Granada (1492), and the nationalistic temper aroused by the ejection of the Moors and the glories of discoveries in the new world had a like effect. Hence Italy found herself disunited and weak in the presence of two united and relatively centralized states, each imbued with intense national pride and each having some claim to interfere in Italian affairs. For French and Spanish kings alike had convenient hereditary pretexts for meddling in Naples, and the vigorous popes of the day found both these mighty outsiders useful to call on when troubles arose within the Italian family.

The death of Lorenzo de' Medici (1492), to whose diplomatic skill historians attribute the efficiency of the balance of power previously alluded to, marked the end of Italian independence. The King of France was only too willing to listen to the appeals of Ludovico, Duke of Milan, who sought his support against the Kingdom of Naples, and, once having come into Italy, he indicated how simple a matter its conquest might be, marching unopposed from Milan to Naples, incidentally displacing the Medici and freeing Pisa from the Florentine yoke en route. His entry into Naples was a triumph, though a revolt of the Neapolitan barons and the formation of an Italian coalition against him forced him to return to France. The French were back again in 1499, under Louis XII, and Machiavelli discusses the actions and policies of this monarch in some detail in Chapter III of *The Prince*. Meanwhile the Spaniards were not idle, and in 1503 their victory over the French at the battle of the Garigliano made them masters of the Kingdom of Naples. The early years of the 16th century were given over to the duel between these two powerful foreigners for domination in Italy; with the battle of Pavia (1525) the Spanish won the decision. Italy was not to be free again until the Risorgimento and the triumph of Cavour and Garibaldi in 1860.

In the midst of the struggle between the two powerful contenders, the popes of Machiavelli's time (Alexander VI, Julius II, Leo X, and Clement VII) tried to carve out a solid temporal state for the Church. In this policy Alexander worked through Cesare Borgia, but his work was undone by Julius, who restored Cesare's conquests to the princelings of Romagna. Julius himself was successful in his major undertakings, for he broke the power of the Venetians (at Vailà, 1509) and drove out the French in spite of their celebrated victory at Ravenna (1512). Yet in the nature of things papal policy was bound to end in destruction of the rival Italian states and hence in the long run in strengthening the grip of the foreigner. The result of the vigorous but inconsistent efforts of the Popes was the sack of Rome by the Emperor Charles V in 1527; Clement VII was obliged to take refuge in the Castel St. Angelo and accept the terms dictated by Charles. From that time on, the temporal power of the papacy was, like every other state in Italy, subject to the will of foreign overlords.

Florence, a wealthy and unarmed state of merchants, a golden-fleeced lamb, as it were, among ravening wolves, reacted sharply to the rapidly succeeding variations of those turbulent times. On the death of Lorenzo, Piero de'

Medici, his eldest son, succeeded but remained only two years in power. The zeal for reform among the people, inspired by the monk Savonarola and his followers, was directed against the Medici, who symbolized in the eyes of the fanatical Dominican both tyranny and immorality. Further complications were added by the approach of Charles VIII, riding in triumph on his road to Naples. Piero was obliged to go out and treat with the French king and to make a number of concessions to him, including a large indemnity and an invitation to occupy the city. On his return from his negotiations with Charles, Piero found the gates of the Palazzo Comunale locked against him and the people, crying "Popolo e libertà," unwilling to receive him. He and his brother the cardinal fled, and under the leadership of Savonarola the ancient republican government with some liberal reforms was reinstituted. Within a few years, however, the reforming ardor of the Friar wearied the people and finally even drove the tolerant Alexander VI to excommunicate him. He was overthrown and burned in the Piazza della Signoria in 1498. The Republic was carried on under a new government of which Soderini was Gonfaloniere and Machiavelli secretary. This regime lasted until 1512, when the Spanish troops, fighting for the Cardinal Giovanni de' Medici, moved on Florence. The new militia, organized by Machiavelli, fled in panic, and the Medici came in again. For a time all was well but when in 1523 Giulio de' Medici left the city to become Pope (Clement VII) the bad government of his representatives began to irk the Florentines, and the humiliation of the Pope at the hands of Charles gave them opportunity for another revolution. Out of this came the last Florentine Republic. Its life was short but glorious. The Emperor united with the Pope to crush it, and after a heroic siege, which is one of the brightest pages in the city's history, the Republic capitulated in 1530, and a free and independent Florence became only a memory.

On May 3, 1469, the same year that marked the marriage of Isabella of Castile and Ferdinand of Aragon, Niccolò Machiavelli was born in Florence. He came of a family which could trace its descent from the old nobility and which, though not wealthy, was not without means. His father was a lawyer. We have little information about Machiavelli's youth; obviously he was well grounded in

Latin, and one of his own letters tells of his devotion to study. His chance came with the administration that followed the downfall of Savonarola; having served briefly as a minor clerk in the chancery he was appointed (1498) secretary to the Republic, responsible to "the Ten" whose concerns were war and internal affairs. Four years later he married Marietta Corsini by whom he had several children. His private letters show that Machiavelli in his lighter moments (which were not infrequent) was given to loose and frivolous conversation, drinking in taverns, and extra-marital love affairs. Nonetheless the marriage seems to have been a happy one.

His new office took him on many diplomatic missions: to Forlì (1499) where he met the indomitable if rather limited Caterina Sforza (*The Prince,* Chap. XX), to France (1500), and to Romagna where (in 1502 and 1503) he had frequent contacts with Cesare Borgia, whom he saw again in Rome later in the latter year. He thus had an opportunity to study this meteoric personage in hours of triumph as well as humiliation. Machiavelli also accompanied Pope Julius II on his march through Umbria and Emilia in 1506, visited the Emperor Maximilian at Bolzano (which he reached by way of Switzerland) in 1508, and was sent on another errand to Louis XII at Blois in 1510. Meanwhile he found time to reorganize the Florentine militia and to offer suggestions for the campaign against Pisa, which fell in 1509.

With the fall of the Republic and the return of the Medici, Machiavelli ceased to be employed by the state. This seems perhaps more natural to us than it did to him. He could not see why his talents were not made use of and made numerous attempts to ingratiate himself with the Medici. While the purity of his patriotism cannot be questioned by any reader of *The Prince,* he seems to have had no ideological convictions, as we should call them nowadays. He was anxious to serve Italy and Florence and not at all concerned with the character of the regime representing them. However he had little success in his efforts to find worthy employment with the Medici, though indeed they seem to have been well disposed to him. Being suspected of conspiracy against the new state, he was tortured and briefly imprisoned but was released on the accession of the Medici Pope Leo X (1513). He was banished from the city for a year but his "exile" was clearly not uncomfortable. He retired to his little estate at San Casciano, not far from Florence, and by 1519 he was already advising the Medici on a new constitution for the city. Later he was given one or two minor charges by Clement VII, one taking him to Lombardy (1526) where he worked with Guicciardini, the other great Florentine historian and at that time the Pope's military delegate. His *History of Florence* is dedicated to Clement. On the expulsion of the Medici in 1527, Machiavelli had high hopes of returning to his old position in the Republic. But just as his services under Soderini had made him suspect to the Medici so his attentions to the latter caused the new Republic to hesitate to enlist him. His old post went to another, and the disappointment may have hastened his end; he died June 22, 1527, a few weeks after the new government was formed. In the Church of Santa Croce in Florence he has been commemorated by a cenotaph bearing the inscription "tanto nomini nullum par elogium."

It is to Machiavelli's enforced seclusion in San Casciano that we owe his more important works. His retirement gave him the opportunity to reread his classics and to study again his beloved Livy. He approached the ancient historians in the true humanistic spirit, pondering and maturing his own conclusions from personal experience in the light of illumination on human affairs provided by the classics. The *Commentary on the first Ten Books of Livy* was begun (apparently in 1512) though not finished till some years after *The Prince,* which is in a sense a chapter of the *Commentary. The Prince* was written in 1513, though it was not published until 1532, five years after the author's death. The *Mandragola* (Mandrake), it seems likely, was also written in this early period of retirement though published only in 1524. This is a lively and mischievous play, the outstanding comedy of the Italian Renaissance, full of realistic observation and having a fast moving plot and crisp dialogue, still capable of pleasing a modern audience. It was in 1520 that Machiavelli was commissioned to write a *History of Florence,* of which the first part, consisting of eight books, was completed in 1525. This work is a monument in historiography for, inspired by Livy, the author attempts not merely to set forth a chronicle of successive events as such histories had hitherto done, but to seek for causes and effects in the sequence of recorded facts. *The Art of War,* in which the author develops his military ideas as outlined in *The Prince,* and the *Life of Castruccio Castracane* appeared in 1520. Other writings of Machiavelli include *Clizia* of the same *genre* as the *Mandragola,* and two other comedies, *Belfagor,* a satire on marriage, and various letters and reports based on his numerous diplomatic missions. Of these the two general reports on France and Germany are still highly readable.

It was *The Prince* that, in the words of Count Carlo Sforza, "made Machiavelli famous and infamous." John Addington Symonds sees in this work "the foundations of modern political science" and points out that the centralized bureaucratic state, typified by France under Louis XIV and Spain under the Hapsburgs, is foreshadowed in this little essay as well as the even more modern system of military conscription. The author's concentration on success and efficiency as the proper goals of government and the cynicism of certain chapters have given him the reputation for unscrupulous cunning and deceit which is still the common connotation of our adjective "Machiavellian." In modern times there has been a tendency to consider Machiavelli more sympathetically; Macaulay finds some justification for his code in the violent and unprincipled character of his age, and others stress his patriotism, which is, to be sure, a kind of idealism. The reader will draw his own conclusions. It is fair to point out that Machiavelli explicitly states that he is not concerned with things as they should be but as experience has shown that they are, and that he is writing on a limited and technical theme: how to be a successful ruler. One would hardly expect a military engineer to be concerned with anything but the effectiveness of his engine; it is his duty to see to it that his tank or his flamethrower really works and for others to determine the uses to which they may be put. It may be true that statecraft has of necessity moral and ethical aspects to which the author of *The Prince* was blind. Yet many a modern reader, looking at the world of today, may well find that Machiavelli's formula for effective and successful government is not so much in need of revision as idealists might wish.

# To the Magnificent Lorenzo, Son of Piero de' Medici

It is the custom of those who are anxious to find favor in the eyes of a prince to present him with such things as they value most highly or in which they see him take delight. Hence offerings are made of horses, arms, golden cloth, precious stones and such ornaments, worthy of the greatness of the Prince. Since therefore I am desirous of presenting myself to Your Magnificence with some token of my eagerness to serve you, I have been able to find nothing in what I possess which I hold more dear or in greater esteem than the knowledge of the actions of great men which has come to me through a long experience of presentday affairs and continual study of ancient times. And having pondered long and diligently on this knowledge and tested it well, I have reduced it to a little volume which I now send to Your Magnificence. Though I consider this work unworthy of your presence, nonetheless I have much hope that your kindness may find it acceptable, if it be considered that I could offer you no better gift than to give you occasion to learn in a very short space of time all that I have come to have knowledge and understanding of over many years and through many hardships and dangers. I have not adorned the work nor inflated it with lengthy clauses nor pompous or magnificent words, nor added any other refinement or extrinsic ornament wherewith many are wont to advertise or embellish their work, for it has been my wish either that no honor should be given it or that simply the truth of the material and the gravity of the subject should make it acceptable.

I hope it may not be considered presumption if a man of low and humble condition dare to discuss and lay down rules for the government of princes, for, just as a landscape artist stands in the plains to survey the nature of mountains and hills and, to study the character of the lowlands, takes up his stand on the hills, so, to know well the nature of peoples one must be a prince and to know the *nature of princes one must be of the people. Let Your Magnificence then be pleased to accept this little gift in the same spirit in which I send it. If Your Magnificence will read and study it carefully the pages will reveal my most ardent desire that you may attain that summit of greatness which fortune and your other qualities promise you. And if from the peak of that summit Your Magnificence may deign some time to cast down a glance upon these humble places beneath, you will know how undeservedly I suffer a great and continuous malignity of fortune.*

# Chapter I

## TYPES OF MONARCHY
## AND HOW THEY ARE ACQUIRED

All states or dominions, past or present, that have held authority over men, are or have been either republics or monarchies. Monarchies may be either hereditary, having had for many years a succession of rulers from the same family, or new. New ones may be entirely new, as Milan was to Francesco Sforza,* or they may be members added to the hereditary state of the prince who acquires them, as is the Kingdom of Naples to the King of Spain. Such acquired possessions either have been used to life under another prince or have been free, and they are acquired 10 by the new prince by force of his own arms or those of others or they fall to him by fortune or because of his character and ability.

# Chapter II

## HEREDITARY MONARCHIES

I shall omit any discussion of republics as I have discussed them fully elsewhere.[1] I shall concern myself only with monarchies and, following the classification set forth above, I shall discuss how they may be governed and preserved. Hereditary states, then, which are accustomed to the rule of the line of their prince, are much more easily maintained than the new ones for it is sufficient for the prince not to transgress the customs of his predecessors and to meet emergencies as they come. Thus if such a prince

---

* Famous mercenary soldier (1401-1466). Married the daughter of Filippo Visconti and on the latter's death became Duke of Milan (1450).

1. In his commentary on Livy. See Introduction.

10 be normally energetic he will always keep his state unless
some extraordinary and excessive force takes it from him,
and even if he loses it the slightest misfortune to the new
ruler will suffice to give it back to him. For example, we
have in Italy the Dukes of Ferrara,[2] who were able to withstand the attack of the Venetians in 1484 and that of Pope
Julius in 1510 [3] simply because their line had been long established in that dominion. Since the natural prince has
less cause and less need to give offence, it is logical that he
should be more loved, and, if exceptional vices do not make
20 him hated, it is reasonable that his subjects should be well
disposed toward him, and in the long duration of a rule
the causes and the memories of innovations are blurred
whereas one change invariably lays the groundwork for
another.

# Chapter III

## MIXED MONARCHIES

It is in the new monarchies that difficulties are found.
First, if it is not wholly new but a part of a state which we
may term mixed, its disorders arise at first from a natural
difficulty common to all new monarchies, for men like to
change their masters, hoping to improve their lot; this
makes them take arms against their rulers only to be disil-
lusioned when they later see by experience that they have
worsened their state. This springs from another simple
and natural cause, which makes it inevitable for a new
10 prince to offend his subjects both by his soldiery and by an
infinite number of other injuries consequent to his new
annexation. Thus you find all whom you have injured in
occupying your new dominion are your enemies, and you
cannot keep as friends those who put you in power since

2. Ercole I in 1484, Alfonso I in 1510, both of the House of Este,
dominant in Ferrara since the middle of the 12th century.
3. Giuliano della Rovere (1443-1513, proclaimed Pope in 1503).
An able diplomat and soldier, he formed the League of Cambrai,
an alliance of the Papacy, France, Spain, and the Empire against
Venice (1508), and the Holy League against the French (1511).
Also carried out reforms within the Church, founded the Vatican
Museum and was patron of Bramante, Raphael, and Michelangelo.

you will be unable to give them the satisfactions they had hoped for, nor can you use strong measures against them as you are under obligation to them, because however strong your army may be you will always need the good will of the inhabitants to enter into a province. For these reasons Louis XII,[1] King of France, occupied Milan in a very short space of time and as quickly lost it. And the first time the forces of Ludovico[2] alone were sufficient to take it from him, for those who had opened their doors to Louis, finding themselves disappointed in him and in the hopes of advantages that they had formed, could not tolerate the tyrannies of their new prince. It is indeed true that when rebellious territories are taken a second time they are not lost so easily, for the master is now, because of the rebellion, not so reluctant to assure his safety by punishing the delinquent, unmasking the suspect, and fortifying his weak spots. So that if the first time the demonstration of Duke Ludovico on the borders was sufficient to cause France the loss of Milan, the second time it took all the world in arms against the French and the utter defeat and ejection from Italy of their armies to regain the city. This was a result of the above mentioned causes. However, he did lose the city both times, and since we have set forth the general causes of the first loss we must now examine those of the second and consider what remedies the King had, or what would be suitable to anyone in his position, in order to preserve his acquisition as France failed to do.

I will point out here that those states which by acquisition are joined to a hereditary possession of their conqueror are either of the same region and language or they are not. When they are, it is very simple to keep them, especially when they have not been used to free government, and to possess them securely all that is needed is that the line of their own princes should become extinct. For, in other matters, preserving their old ways and finding no difference in customs, men will live in quiet. This can be seen in the case of Burgundy, Brittany, Gascony, and Normandy, which have been so long attached to France, and

---

1. 1462-1515, crowned 1499. Called "father of the people."
2. 1451-1508. Called "il Moro," son of Francesco Sforza. Ruled Milan from 1494 to 1500. Driven out by the French in 1499, he returned briefly to be permanently deposed the following year. Patron of Leonardo da Vinci.

though among them there is some lack of uniformity in language, yet their customs are similar and thus they get on well together. But a prince who makes an annexation of this sort and wishes to keep it must have two considerations in mind: he must be sure that the line of the ancient princes is extinct and he must refrain from changing the laws or taxes of his new subjects; thus in a short while the 60 latter will become completely identified with his hereditary principality. But when possessions are acquired in a province differing in language, customs, and laws, there are difficulties, and it takes great good luck and energy to keep them. One of the best and most effective means would be for the person who acquires them to go and live in them; this would make possession of them more secure and enduring. This is what the Turk has done in Greece. And if he had not done so he would not have been able to hold that state in spite of all the other measures he has adopted to 70 that end. For, being on the spot, one can see disorders as they arise and can quickly take measures against them, but from a distance they are heard of only when they are already grave, and it is too late to take measures. Further, the province is not despoiled by your officials, and the subjects can get satisfaction by immediate appeal to the prince whence if they wish to be good subjects they have greater cause to love him and if they wish otherwise, to fear him. And if anyone from outside considers an attack on that state he has reason to hesitate, for a prince dwelling therein 80 is more difficult to dislodge.

Another good plan is to send colonies into one or two key places of the new province; indeed it is necessary either to do this or to maintain in such places large bodies of armed men. The prince will not spend much on colonies and can send them out and maintain them at little or no expense. With them he injures only those whose fields and houses he takes away to give to the colonists, and these are a very small minority of his new state. Since those thus injured are scattered and few in number, they can do the 90 prince no harm, and the other inhabitants, having suffered no loss, are easy to keep quiet and are also careful to behave well so that they may not share the fate of those that have had their property taken from them. So to sum up: such colonies are inexpensive, they are loyal, and they cause little harm, and the injured persons being few and scattered can give no trouble, as I have said. For it is to be noted that men must be either conciliated or annihilated; for they take vengeance for slight injuries while for the grave ones they cannot. Hence the injury done to a man must be of such a nature as to make vengeance impossible. 100

But if, instead of colonies, soldiers have to be maintained, the cost is much greater as the income from the new state will be eaten up by the expense of policing it, so that the acquisition turns out to be an expense. Besides, such a measure is much more offensive for it is harmful to the whole state, as the discomfort of an occupying army is felt by all and so everyone becomes its enemy, and such enemies can do much harm, even though beaten, on their own ground. Under every aspect then, garrisons are useless, and colonies are useful. 110

Further, one who finds himself in this alien type of province must make himself a leader and defender of his less powerful neighbors and strive to weaken the stronger ones and see to it that under no circumstances a foreign prince as powerful as himself comes into the province. If a foreigner gets in, it will always be because he is encouraged by those within the country who are disaffected through fear or ambition. This was seen long ago in the case of the Aetolians who brought the Romans into Greece, and in every other province the latter entered they were brought 120 in by the inhabitants. The rule of the matter is this: as soon as a powerful foreigner enters a country, all the less powerful of that country join him, moved by envy of those who have ruled over them; so, he has no difficulties at all in attracting them, for immediately and willingly they attach themselves to the state he has acquired. He has only to take care lest they gain too much strength or authority and then with their favor and his own strength he can easily put down those who are powerful and thus remain in all things the arbiter of the province. He who fails to govern 130 well in this matter will soon lose whatever he has won and even while he holds it will have infinite trouble and annoyances.

The Romans, in the provinces they took, followed such a course and sent out colonies, attracted the less powerful without increasing their power, put down the powerful, and allowed no strong foreigners to win prestige. Their dealings in Greece alone are examples enough. They accepted the Achaeans and the Aetolians, they overthrew the kingdom of the Macedonians and drove out Antiochus; the merits of the Aetolians and Achaeans were never deemed great enough to permit them to add to their holdings, the pleas of Philip never persuaded the Romans to befriend him until they had lowered his standing, and the power of Antiochus did not avail to make them consent to his holding any part of that province. The Romans in these matters acted as all wise princes should, having regard not only to present ills but to future ones as well and preparing for the latter with all possible care. For if evils are anticipated they can easily be remedied but if you wait till they come to you the remedy is too late and the sickness is past cure, such things being like the hectic fever which, as the doctors tell us, at first is easy to cure though hard to recognize, but in time, if it has not been diagnosed and treated, becomes easy to recognize and hard to cure. This is true of affairs of state, for if the ills that are shaping up in the present are recognized in advance (and this is an art possessed only by the prudent) they can be quickly remedied, but if, not being recognized, they are allowed to grow until they are evident to all, there is no longer any remedy. So the Romans, foreseeing difficulties still in the distance, always had a remedy for them, and they never allowed them to grow in order to avoid a war, for they knew that a war cannot be avoided but only put off to the enemy's advantage. On this account they were willing to make war on Philip and Antiochus in Greece rather than have to fight them in Italy though at the time they could have avoided either course. This they chose not to do, nor did they ever esteem that maxim always on the lips of our modern sages who speak of "playing for time," but chose rather to follow the dictates of their own courage and good sense, for time brings all things, bad as well as good.

But to return to France, let us see if she did any of the things we have mentioned. I shall speak of Louis and not Charles [3] for as the former has held possessions in Italy for a longer time, his actions can be better studied and you will see that he did just the opposite to what should have been done to preserve an alien acquisition. King Louis was brought into Italy by the ambition of the Venetians, who

3. Charles VIII (1470-1498, ruled from 1483). See Introduction.

wanted to win half the state of Lombardy by his coming. 180
I do not wish to blame the King for this kind of entry or
the rôle he played because, desirous as he was of getting a
foothold in Italy and having no friends in this country—
indeed on account of Charles' behavior all doors were
closed to him—he was obliged to take what friends he
could find. And his plans would have met with speedy success had he made no mistakes in his other actions. Once he
had occupied Lombardy, then, he regained all the prestige
lost by Charles; Genoa yielded, the Florentines became
friends, the Marquis of Mantua, the Duke of Ferrara, the 190
Bentivogli,[4] the Lady of Forlì and the Lords of Faenza,
Pesaro, Rimini, Camerino, and Piombino, the people of
Lucca, Pisa, Siena—everyone in fact, came forward to offer him friendship and at that point the Venetians might
well have reflected on the rashness of their decision for,
just to gain two towns in Lombardy they had made the
King the master of two-thirds of Italy. Consider now how
easily the King might have maintained his position in
Italy if he had followed the rules set forth above, affording
safety and protection to his friends who, being numerous 200
and weak and fearful, some of the Church, others of the Venetians, were bound to stand by him, thus easily making
him safe against such states as still remained powerful.

Yet hardly was he in Milan, when he adopted just the
contrary course, assisting Pope Alexander [5] in the occupation of Romagna. Nor did it occur to him that in so doing
he weakened himself, shaking off his friends and those
who had turned to him for protection, and strengthened
the Church, adding the temporal to its spiritual power by
which it has so much authority. And having made one mis- 210
take he had to follow it with another when, in order to
check the ambition of Alexander and prevent him from becoming master of Tuscany, he was forced to come into
Italy. And still it was not enough for him to have strengthened the Church and alienated his friends; his desire for
the Kingdom of Naples led him to partition it with the
King of Spain,[6] thus, where he had been sole arbiter, cre-

4. of Bologna.
5. Roderigo Borgia (1431-1503). Made Pope in 1492. Father of
Cesare and Lucrezia Borgia. Artful diplomat, ambitious for his family
and the temporal power of the Church.
6. Ferdinand of Aragon (1452-1516). See Introduction.

ating a peer, so that the ambitious of that realm who were dissatisfied with him might have elsewhere to turn, and where he could have left in that Kingdom a King who would be his own pensioner, removing him and setting up one who could dispossess him.

It is a normal and natural thing to want to acquire possessions, and when men who can, do acquire they will receive praise and not blame, but when they cannot and yet strive to acquire at any cost, herein lies the blameworthy mistake. So that if France with her own forces could have attacked Naples she should have done so and if she could not, she should not have divided it. And if the partition of Lombardy with the Venetians is excusable as giving a foothold in Italy, the partition of Naples, not having that justification, is to be criticized. Louis, then, made these five errors: he ruined the less powerful states, he increased the power in Italy of one already strong, he brought into the country a most powerful foreigner, he did not come to live in the country himself, he did not plant colonies in it. Yet all these mistakes, as long as he lived, might not have hurt him if he had not committed a sixth, which was to deprive the Venetians of their State. For if he had not strengthened the Church nor brought Spain into Italy it would have been reasonable and necessary to humble the Venetians but as he had adopted the line of action that he did, he should never have consented to their downfall, since, as long as they remained strong they would have kept the others from attacking Lombardy, both because they would not have agreed unless they themselves were to be masters there, and because the others would not have been disposed to take it from France to give it to them and would not have had the courage to attack both.

And if it is said that Louis yielded Romagna to the Pope and Naples to Spain to avoid war, I answer that one should not accept disorder to avoid war, for, as noted above, a war is never avoided but merely postponed to your own disadvantage. And if another refers to the pledge given by the King to the Pope to undertake this enterprise in return for the annulment of his marriage [7] and the cardinalship

7. Louis XII divorced his first wife Joanne in order to marry the widow of Charles VIII and thus retain possession of Brittany. Alexander VI gave his consent.

of Rouen [8] I will answer with what I shall have to say later concerning the faith of princes and how it should be kept. So that King Louis lost Lombardy because he did not observe any of those rules followed by others who were bent on maintaining the provinces they had acquired. There is nothing miraculous about this, it is perfectly natural and normal. On this matter I spoke with the Cardinal de Rouen at Nantes when Valentino (as Cesare Borgia,[9] the son of Pope Alexander, was popularly called) was occupying Romagna. Cardinal de Rouen told me then that Italians knew nothing of warfare and I replied that the French knew nothing of statecraft for if they did they would not have allowed the Church to become so great. And we have now seen by experience that the greatness in Italy of both the Church and Spain was caused by the French, whose downfall was brought about by them. Whence we can draw the general rule, almost never broken: whoever is the cause of another's coming to power, falls himself, for that power is built up either by art or force, both of which are suspect to the one who has become powerful.

8. George d'Amboise (1460-1510), Archbishop of Rouen, created Cardinal by Alexander VI. Advisor and minister of Louis XII.

9. Created Archbishop of Valencia in 1492 and Cardinal the following year, Cesare was released from his ecclesiastical duties in 1498 and sent to France as papal legate carrying the bull annulling Louis' marriage. On this occasion he was made Duc de Valentinois and a year later married the sister of the King of Navarre. See following chapters for his activities in Romagna. On accession of Julius II he lost his conquests and was compelled to leave Italy. Killed in a skirmish in Spain (1476-1507).

# Chapter IV

## WHY THE KINGDOM OF DARIUS, OCCUPIED
## BY ALEXANDER, DID NOT REBEL
## AGAINST ALEXANDER'S
## SUCCESSORS AFTER
## HIS DEATH

In view of the difficulties of holding a newly acquired state some may wonder about the conquest of Alexander the Great. He made himself master of Asia within a few years and had hardly taken possession of it when he died, whence it would have seemed reasonable for the new state to rebel. Yet in fact, his successors kept it for themselves and had no difficulties in holding it save those that were born of their own rivalries. By way of answer let me say that all monarchies we have any knowledge of have been
10 governed in one of two ways, either by one Prince with all others as his servants, who, acting as his ministers, through his favor and permission, assist in governing the kingdom, or by a prince and a number of barons who hold their rank not by favor of the sovereign but by the antiquity of their line. Such barons have states and subjects of their own, who recognize them as lords and have a natural allegiance to them. The states governed by a Prince and his servants accord greater authority to their prince because in all his domain none is recognized as superior save him and when
20 they obey another it is only as a minister or an official to whom they feel no particular devotion.

The Turk and the King of France exemplify these two kinds of government in our day. The whole monarchy of the Turk is governed by one master; the rest are his servants and, dividing his kingdom into sanjaks he sets up different administrators therein and changes them at his pleasure. But the King of France finds himself in the midst of a great number of established lords, acknowledged and beloved of their subjects; they have their privileges which
30 the king may not take from them without danger to himself. Whoever studies these two kinds of states will find

the state of the Turk difficult to conquer but, once conquered, very easy to hold. The reasons for the difficulty in
conquering the state of the Turk is that the invader cannot
be called in by the princes of that kingdom nor can he hope
his enterprise will be facilitated by the rebellion of those
the monarch has about him since, as we have indicated
above, all being servants and under obligation to their lord,
they are difficult to corrupt and even if corrupted would be
of little use since they cannot bring their people with them. 40
Thus, anyone planning to attack the Turk must expect to
find a united state and must hope more in his own strength
than in the dissension of others, yet once the Turk is beaten
and broken in battle and unable to reform his armies there
is nothing more to fear save from the family of the prince
himself and once his line were extinct there would be no
one else to fear since no other has prestige among the people from whom, as the victor would have nothing to hope
before the occupation, he would have nothing to fear after.

In monarchies governed as France is, the contrary is 50
true. You can always find it easy to get in by winning over
some barons of the realm, for there are always malcontents
and those desiring a change. Such persons can open the
way for you, for the reasons above noted, and can assist
you in victory. But after that, if you wish to hold your acquisition, infinite troubles arise both from those who have
helped you and those oppressed by you. Nor is it enough to
see to it that the line of the prince becomes extinct, for the
barons remain and become leaders in new uprisings and
since you cannot either satisfy or annihilate them all, you 60
will lose the state whenever the occasion presents itself.

Now, if you will consider the nature of the government
of Darius you will find it similar to the kingdom of the
Turk, and hence Alexander at first had to break it completely and sweep the King from the field and then, Darius
dead, the state remained firmly in Alexander's hands for
the reasons set forth above. And had his successors remained united they would have been able to enjoy it at
their ease for in that kingdom no disorders arose save the
ones they created themselves. 70

But states constituted like France are impossible to hold
with such ease. The frequent revolts against the Romans
in Spain, France, and Greece were occasioned by the numerous principalities in those states, for, as long as the

memory of them endured, the Romans were insecure in their rule, but once the memory of these principalities had grown dim the power and duration of the Roman Empire assured them of their possession. Later, in the quarrels among themselves, each of the Roman leaders could count
80 on support from those provinces in proportion to his authority within them, and once the line of their ancient lords had become extinct they recognized no others save the Romans. No one will wonder then, considering these things, that Alexander found it easy to hold the realm of Asia, nor that others found it difficult to preserve their gains, as Pyrrhus and many more; this was not a result of the greater or less ability of the conqueror but rather of the differences between the countries occupied.

# Chapter V

## HOW CITIES OR STATES PREVIOUSLY INDEPENDENT MUST BE GOVERNED AFTER OCCUPATION

When those states which have been accustomed to live in freedom under their own laws are acquired, there are three ways of trying to keep them. The first is to destroy them, the second to go and live therein, and the third to allow them to continue to live under their own laws, taking a tribute from them and creating within them a new government of a few which will keep the state friendly to you. For since such a government is the creature of the prince it will know that it cannot exist without his friend-
10 ship and authority and is thus certain to do its best to support him, and a city accustomed to freedom can be more easily held through its citizens than in any other way if it is desired to preserve it. Here we have the examples of the Spartans and the Romans. The Spartans held Athens and Thebes and created in both a government of a few; nonetheless they lost them. The Romans, in order to hold Capua, Carthage, and Numantia, razed them and did not lose them. They tried to keep Greece in the same way the

Spartans had, permitting the country to be free under its own laws, but in this they were not successful inasmuch 20 as they were compelled to destroy many cities of that province in order to hold it, for in truth there is no sure way of holding them other than by their ruin. And whoever becomes master of a city accustomed to living in freedom and does not destroy it may expect to be destroyed by it himself, for it has always as an incentive to rebellion the name of liberty and its own ancient laws which neither time nor favors received can cause the citizens to forget. And whatever action be taken or provision be made, as long as the inhabitants are not separated or dispersed, that name and 30 those laws are never forgotten but provide a rallying point in every emergency, as is shown by the case of Pisa [1] after many years of subjection to the Florentines. Cities or provinces used to living under a prince are accustomed to obedience, and when the ruling house becomes extinct they are unable to agree on a successor and, having no experience of self-government, they are slow in taking up arms and so with greater ease a prince may overcome them and feel secure in his possession of them. In republics there is greater life, greater hatred, more desire of vengeance, and 40 the memory of their ancient liberty gives them no rest; so the safest way is either to extinguish them or go and live in them.

# Chapter VI

## OF NEW MONARCHIES ACQUIRED BY ONE'S OWN ARMS AND ABILITY

Let no one be surprised if, in what I have to say of new monarchies both as regarding the prince and the state, I adduce great examples; for men almost always follow the paths beaten by others and imitate their actions, yet, being unable to follow exactly the same line and unequal in character to those whom he imitates, a prudent man should al-

1. Pisa had fallen to the Florentines in 1406. The city took advantage of the invasion of Charles VIII to reassert its independence and maintained it against repeated sieges by the Florentines until 1509.

ways walk in the path marked by great men and imitate those who have been preeminent, so that if his ability does not allow him to rise to their height it may at least show
10 some likeness to them. Thus he will do as prudent archers who, when they find their target too distant and knowing how far the strength of their bow will carry, aim much higher than the mark, not indeed to reach such a height with their strength or their arrow but in order to be able, with such a high aim to hit the assigned spot. To continue then: in entirely new monarchies where there is a new prince there will be found fewer or more difficulties in holding them according to whether he who rules them is more or less able. And since becoming a prince from pri-
20 vate station presupposes either character or fortune it would seem that either the one or the other of these gifts should in part mitigate many difficulties. Nevertheless, it has happened that those who have owed less to fortune have held on more successfully. Greater ease is also assured by the prince being compelled, for lack of other possessions, to come and live in his new province.

But to come to those who through their own ability and not through fortune have become princes, I shall cite as the most excellent Moses, Cyrus, Romulus, Theseus, and
30 the like. And though we should not speak of Moses, as he was merely an agent of things ordained by God, he yet deserves our admiration if only through the special grace which allowed him to speak with God. But observing Cyrus and the others who acquired or founded kingdoms, we shall see that they are all admirable, and if we study their particular measures and actions they will be found not unlike those of Moses though he had so great a Preceptor. And examining their lives and deeds we shall see that they got nothing from fortune save the occasions which gave
40 them the opportunity of introducing the forms of government which they thought best. Without opportunity their valor and wisdom would have been of no avail and without their talents the opportunity would have been missed. For Moses it was necessary that he should find the people of Israel in Egypt enslaved and oppressed by the Egyptians, so that they should be willing to follow him in order to escape from servitude. To have Romulus become king and founder of Rome it was necessary that he should be unable to live in Alba and be exposed at birth. Cyrus had to find

the Persians discontented with the rule of the Medes and
the latter weak and effeminate from a long period of peace.
Nor could Theseus have exhibited his talents if he had not
found the Athenians dispersed. Such opportunities were
lucky for these men, and their own native abilities seized
the occasion whence their countries were ennobled and
made happy.

Those who become princes by valorous conduct like men
of this sort find it difficult to win their realm but they keep
it without trouble, and the difficulties of acquisition are occasioned in part by the new measures and methods which
they are obliged to introduce in order to found the state
and make themselves secure. It must be remembered that
there is nothing more difficult to plan, more doubtful of
success, nor more dangerous to manage than the creation
of a new system. For the initiator has the enmity of all who
would profit by the preservation of the old institutions and
merely lukewarm defenders in those who would gain by
the new ones. The hesitation of the latter arises in part
from the fear of their adversaries, who have the laws on
their side, and in part from the general skepticism of mankind which does not really believe in an innovation until
experience proves its value. So it happens that whenever
his enemies have occasion to attack the innovator they do
so with the passion of partisans while the others defend
him sluggishly so that the innovator and his party are alike
vulnerable.

On this subject it is further necessary to inquire whether
such innovators can rely on their own strength or must depend on others, that is, whether they must ask help of others to carry on their work or can use force. In the first case
they always come to a bad end and accomplish nothing
but when they can depend on their own strength and are
able to use force they rarely fail. Hence all armed prophets
have been successful and all the unarmed have come to
ruin, for, besides the other reasons adduced, the nature of
peoples is fickle, and it is easy to persuade them of something but difficult to keep them in that persuasion. And so
it is best to have matters ordered in such a way that when
people no longer believe in the innovation they can be compelled to believe by force. Moses, Cyrus, Theseus, and
Romulus could not long have secured the observance of
their new constitutions if they had been without arms; we

have in our own times the case of the monk Girolamo Savonarola,[1] who was himself swept away with all his new measures as soon as the multitude ceased to have faith in him, for he had no means of keeping faithful those who had believed in him nor of forcing the dissident to conform. Such leaders meet with great difficulties and all their dangers confront them on their way to power and must be overcome by their talents, but once such dangers are overcome and they come to be held in veneration, having done away with those envious of them, they remain powerful, secure, honored, and happy. I should like to add to such lofty examples another of lesser magnitude, yet having some resemblance to the first and sufficient to exemplify this class. This is Hiero of Syracuse, who from the status of a private citizen became prince of his city. Fortune merely provided him with the occasion, for the Syracusans, being oppressed, chose him as their captain and his merits then made him their prince. And his private character was such that one writing of him says that he lacked nothing a king should have save only a kingdom. He disbanded the old army and created a new one and put aside his old friendships and took up new ones and when he had friends and soldiers of his own he was able to build on this foundation; thus it cost him much labor to acquire, but little to preserve.

# Chapter VII

## NEW MONARCHIES ACQUIRED BY THE POWER OF OTHERS OR BY FORTUNE

Those who rise from a private station to rulership merely by fortune have few difficulties in their ascent but many in retaining their position. The path upward is easy for they fly, and all the difficulties begin after they have achieved their distinction. In this class we may place those who are awarded a state either for money or as a favor from the giver, as happened to many in Greece in the cities of Ionia and the Hellespont when they were made princes

1. See Introduction.

by Darius in order that they might hold those lands for
his safety and glory. Of like sort were those emperors who   10
came to the purple from the condition of simple citizens
through corruption of the soldiery. Princes of this stamp
depend absolutely on the will or fortune of those who have
raised them up, and both are unreliable and insecure foundations. They have neither the knowledge nor the ability
to preserve their rank; they do not know enough because
it is not likely that one who has always lived as a private
citizen, unless he be of rare wit and character, will know
how to command; they cannot because they have no forces
of their own well disposed and faithful to them. Further,   20
states which spring up suddenly, like all other things in
nature quick in birth and growth, cannot have roots and
connections and are uprooted by the first adverse wind,
unless, as we have remarked, those who have so suddenly
become princes are men of such character as will know how
immediately to prepare for the preservation of what fortune has dropped in their laps, and how to lay such foundations to their state after their elevation as other princes
make before.

As examples of these two ways of becoming a prince—    30
either through talent or fortune—I shall mention two
names of our own time: Francesco Sforza and Cesare Borgia. Francesco by the proper means and through his own
ability rose from private station to be Duke of Milan and
preserved with little effort the duchy which had cost him
many pains to acquire. On the other hand, Cesare Borgia,
commonly called Valentino, won his state by the fortune of
his father and lost it in the same way, in spite of putting
forth every effort and doing everything that a prudent and
able man should do to lodge himself firmly in the state in   40
which the arms and fortune of another had placed him. For,
as we have said above, if the foundations are not laid be-
forehand, it is possible to lay them afterwards granting
unusual ability, even though they are thus laid with incon-
venience to the architect and danger to the edifice. And if
we examine the procedure of the Duke we shall see what
strong foundations he had laid for future power; this is, I
think, not out of place in our discussion for I could not suggest better precepts to a new prince than the examples of
Cesare's actions. And if his measures did not avail him it   50

was not his fault but the result of an unusually and extremely malignant fortune.

Alexander VI, seeking to aggrandize his son, encountered many difficulties both present and future. First, he saw no way of making him lord of any state save one of the Church, and, casting about to seize a state of the Church, he knew that the Duke of Milan and the Venetians would not permit it because Faenza and Rimini were already under the protection of the Venetians. Further he saw that the armies of Italy, especially those that might be useful to him, were under the command of men such as the Orsini and Colonna, who were bound to fear the greatness of the Pope, and therefore he could not trust them. To make himself master over part of Italy, it was necessary to change these conditions and create disorder among the Italian states. This the Pope found easy to do, as the Venetians, for other reasons, had already taken steps to bring the French back into Italy, and Alexander, far from opposing their project, facilitated it by the annulment of the first marriage of King Louis. Thus the King came into Italy with the aid of the Venetians and the consent of the Pope, and no sooner was he in Milan than the Pope got from him troops for his enterprise in Romagna which he won by the prestige of the King.

Now when the Duke had thus acquired Romagna and beaten the Colonna he wished to preserve his winnings and go further, but two considerations gave him pause: for one thing he was not sure of the troops he commanded and for another he could not count on the good will of France. That is to say, he was afraid the troops of the Orsini that he had employed might fail him and not only make further gains impossible but even take from him what he had won, and he feared a like conduct on the part of the King of France. He had some indication of the attitude of the Orsini for after the storming of Faenza he found them very cool in the attack on Bologna when he moved on that city. As for the King, he learned his intentions when, having taken the Duchy of Urbino, he attacked Tuscany and had the King ask him to abandon that enterprise. Whereupon the Duke determined to be no longer dependent on the fortune or arms of others. And his first action was to weaken the Orsini and Colonna parties in Rome. He won over all their adherents of rank and attached them to himself, giving them large allowances and honoring them with commands or offices according to their station, so that within a few months all the devotion they had felt for their parties was gone and had been placed instead in the Duke. After this he waited for a chance to crush the Orsini, having already broken up the party of the Colonna. The chance when it came was good and his use of it better. The Orsini, 100 realizing tardily that the greatness of the Duke and the Church signified ruin for them, summoned a diet in La Magione near Perugia. This was the cause of the rebellion of Urbino and the disorders in Romagna and of infinite perils to the Duke himself. He overcame them all with the help of the French, and, having reestablished his prestige and no longer trusting in France nor any strength but his own, in order not to take any chances he turned to dissimulation. And he knew so well how to hide his real intentions that the Orsini were reconciled with him through the in- 110 tervention of Signor Paolo, whom the Duke spared no effort to win over, presenting him with robes, money, and horses. So in their simplicity they all were induced to come to Sinigaglia and fell into his hands. Thus doing away with the leaders and making their followers his friends, the Duke had laid very good foundations for his power, having all Romagna and the Duchy of Urbino and having won over the people of those regions with their first taste of the advantages of his rule.

The last item is worthy of note and of imitation by oth- 120 ers, and I do not wish to pass over it. When the Duke had taken Romagna he found it had been governed by weak rulers, who had rather preyed on their subjects than governed them, giving them more motive for disunion than union, so much so indeed that the province was rife with robberies, feuds, and all kinds of lawlessness. To make it peaceful and obedient to his rule, he judged it necessary to give it a good government. To this end he appointed Messer Remiro d'Orco, a cruel and energetic man, as governor, giving him full powers. This official, to his own 130 great renown, soon made the province peaceful and united. Then the Duke, judging that such excessive authority was no longer needed as he feared that it might become odious, set up a civil court of justice in the middle of the province with an excellent president and a representative from each city. And being aware that the recent harshness had

aroused some hatred against him, and wishing to purge the minds of the people and win them over to him without reserve, he decided to make it apparent that if there had
140 been any cruelty it was not his responsibility but had resulted from the harsh temperament of his minister. And taking advantage of the occasion he had this official cut in two pieces one morning and exposed on the public square of Cesena with a piece of wood and a bloody knife by his side. This ferocious spectacle left the people at once content and horrified.

But returning to our subject: when the Duke found himself quite powerful and in part protected from present dangers by having armed himself to his own taste, and to a
150 great extent swept away such armies as were close enough to do him harm, he saw that if he wished to proceed with his conquests he had only the French to consider, for he knew that he would get no further support from the King of France, who had finally perceived his error. So he began to look for new friends and when the French marched towards the Kingdom of Naples to attack the Spanish besieging Gaeta he gave them only wavering support. His purpose was to assure himself of them and in this he would have succeeded if Alexander had lived. Such were his
160 measures as regards pressing matters. And as to the future he had first of all to consider that a new Pope might not be friendly to him and might indeed try to take from him what Alexander had given him. And he had four remedies in mind. First, he planned on extinguishing the line of all the lords he had despoiled so that the new Pope might not have such pretexts at hand. Secondly, he thought to win over all the people of rank in Rome so that through them he might hold the Pope in check. Thirdly, as far as practicable he would control the College of Cardinals.
170 Fourthly, he would seek to get as much power as possible before the death of Alexander and thus be in a position to resist the first shock. And of these four projects he had already accomplished three and was well on his way to the accomplishing of the fourth when Alexander died. Of the lords he had despoiled he had killed as many as he could lay hands on, and very few were left; he had succeeded in winning over the nobility of Rome and had assured himself of a large majority in the College of Cardinals. As for adding to his power, he had planned to make himself master

of Tuscany, and Perugia and Piombino were already in 180
his hands and Pisa under his protection. And when he no
longer had to pay heed to the French (which became un-
necessary when the French lost Naples to the Spaniards so
that both parties needed his friendship) he was ready to
pounce on Pisa. Then Lucca and Siena would quickly have
yielded, partly out of hatred of Florence and partly out of
fear. There would then have been no hope for the Florentines and had he succeeded (and the matter was in hand the
very year that Alexander died) he would have acquired
such strength and prestige that he would have been able 190
to stand on his own feet, dependent only on his own power
and skill and not on the forces or fortunes of another. But
Alexander died only five years after the Duke had first
drawn his sword, and Valentino was left with the state of
Romagna well consolidated but all the rest still in the making, placed between two very powerful hostile armies and
himself sick unto death. Yet the Duke was a man of such
savage courage and ability and was so well aware of just
how men are to be won over or ruined, and had laid such
firm foundations within this short time that, had he not 200
had the two armies pressing on him or had he been in
good health, he would have overcome every difficulty. As
an indication of the solidity of his foundations, it is to be
noted that Romagna loyally awaited him for more than a
month, and even though half dead he lived safely in
Rome, and when the Baglioni, Vitelli, and Orsini came to
the city they could not raise a following against him. And
if he could not make a Pope of his own choosing he was
still able to see to it that the man he didn't want failed of
election. So, if he had been in good health at the time of 210
Alexander's death, he would have had no trouble. He told
me himself at the time of the election of Julius II that he
had thought of everything that might happen at his father's death and had found a remedy for everything save
only that he had not expected at such a time to be at the
point of death himself.

Thus, surveying all the actions of the Duke, I can find
nothing with which to reproach him, rather it seems that
I ought to point him out as an example (as I have done)
to all those who have risen to power by fortune or by the 220
arms of others. For, being a man of great spirit and high
aims, he could not have behaved differently, and the only

obstacles to his designs were the shortness of Alexander's life and his own illness. Whoever finds it necessary in the early stages of his rule to make himself secure against enemies and win friends, to be victorious either by force or fraud, to make himself loved and feared by the people and reverenced and obeyed by his troops, to crush those who have reason or power to be dangerous, to refurbish ancient laws with new measures, to be severe and indulgent, magnanimous and liberal, to disband an old untrustworthy army and build up a new one, to preserve the friendship of kings and princes in such a way that they will give assistance with pleasure and offense with caution: whoever, I repeat, seeks examples in these matters cannot find better ones than in the actions of this man.

He is to be criticized only in the choice of Julius II, which was a bad selection. As we have said, he could not have his own man but he could have prevented the election of any one candidate, and he should never have permitted the election of any of the cardinals whom he had injured or any who might on their election have reason to fear him. For men injure others either through fear or hate. Among those whom he had injured were San Pietro ad Vincula,[1] Colonna, San Giorgio, and Ascanio. All the others, had the choice fallen on them, would have had reason to fear him except Rouen or the Spanish cardinals. The former would have had no reason for fear, being connected with the King of France, and the latter would have been bound to the Duke by relationship and obligations. Hence the Duke should have assured the election of a Spanish Pope and, failing in that, should have accepted Rouen and not San Pietro ad Vincula. For whoever thinks that in great personages present favors erase the memory of past injuries is mistaken. Thus the Duke erred in this election, and it was the cause of his ultimate ruin.

1. Della Rovere, later Julius II.

# Chapter VIII

## ON THOSE WHO HAVE BECOME PRINCES BY CRIME

Since there are two ways in which a man may rise from private station to rulership not entirely because of fortune or ability I do not wish to omit them, although of one it would be possible to speak more fully if we were discussing republics. These are: the ascent to power through crime and wicked conduct, and the elevation of a private citizen to government of his country through the choice of his fellow citizens.

To speak of the first sort I shall illustrate it with two examples, one ancient and one modern, and shall go into no further detail on its merits, since the examples will suffice for any who have need of imitating them. The Sicilian Agathocles rose to be king of Syracuse not merely from private station but from a most base and abject origin. The son of a potter, he led a most wicked life through all the stages of his fortune. However, his wickedness was accompanied by such mental and physical qualities that he rose through the ranks of the militia to be praetor of Syracuse. When he was secure in this rank, he made up his mind to become a prince and to hold by force and without obligation to others what had been given him by agreement. Having informed Hamilcar the Carthaginian of this plan (for the latter was campaigning in Sicily with his armies), he convoked the people and the senate of Syracuse one morning as if he had to discuss matters affecting the republic and, at a given signal, had all the senators and rich men of the people killed by his soldiers. With them out of the way he assumed and retained the lordship of the city without any controversy. And although he was twice defeated in battle and finally even besieged by the Carthaginians he was nonetheless able not merely to defend his city but even to assault Africa with a body of his troops while leaving others as a garrison and thus to raise the siege of Syracuse in a very short time and to press the Carthaginians so hard that they had to come to terms with him and be satisfied to keep Africa and leave Sicily to him.

Studying the actions and talents of Agathocles, one can see little or nothing that can be attributed to fortune inasmuch as he came to power—as we have noted—by no one's favor but through the ranks of the militia, earning his advancement in a thousand dangers and hardships, and held on to his power with the lively and dangerous devices we have mentioned. Nor can we attribute to valor such acts as the killing of his fellow citizens, the betrayal of friends, the lack of loyalty, piety, and religion; for such things win authority but not glory. Yet, if we consider the courage of Agathocles in confronting and surmounting dangers and the greatness of his spirit in enduring and overcoming adversities, it is hard to see why he should be held inferior to any excellent captain. Nevertheless, his excessive cruelty and inhumanity and his infinite crimes do not allow us to include him among men of real excellence. Hence we cannot attribute to fortune or valor an acquisition made without either.

In our own times, in the papacy of Alexander VI we have the case of Oliverotto da Fermo. He had been left an orphan and was brought up by a maternal uncle, Giovanni Fogliani. In his early youth he was sent to serve in the troops of Paolo Vitelli so that he might profit by the discipline and attain to high rank in his army. After the death of Paolo he served under the latter's brother, Vitellozzo, and in a short time, because he was clever and dashing in person and wit, he became one of the foremost leaders of the troops. Then, as it seemed to him humiliating to serve under others, he conceived with Vitelli's approval the idea of occupying Fermo by the aid of some citizens of the town to whom servitude was more dear than the liberty of their city. So he wrote to Giovanni Fogliani that, having been several years away from home, he was now desirous of seeing his uncle and his native town and looking over his estate. And he added that since all his efforts had been spent in the pursuit of honor, in order that his fellow citizens might see that his time had not been spent in vain, he wished to arrive with dignity and accompanied by a hundred horsemen, his friends and servants, and he begged his uncle to be pleased to see that he was honorably received by the citizens of Fermo, for this would not only redound to his credit but to his uncle's as well, since he had been

his ward. And in truth Giovanni in no way failed in showing every honor to his nephew and had him accorded an 80
honorable reception by the people of Fermo and lodged
him and his entourage in his own houses. Here, after some
days had passed, allowing Oliverotto to make preparations
for his crime, he gave a formal banquet to which he
invited Giovanni Fogliani and all the dignitaries of Fermo.
When they had finished the dinner, with the other en-
tertainments that usually accompany such a banquet, Oliverotto artfully brought the conversation around to some
serious matters, speaking of the greatness of Alexander VI
and his son Cesare Borgia and their affairs. When Gio- 90
vanni and the others began to answer and take part in the
discussion, he arose and said that such things were to be
spoken of in a more secret place and withdrew into a cham-
ber, followed by Giovanni and the rest. They had hardly
seated themselves when soldiers came out from behind
hiding places and killed Giovanni and all the others. After
the murders Oliverotto mounted his horse and rode
through the city and besieged the supreme magistrate in
the town hall so that out of fear they were all obliged to
obey him and set up a government of which he was the 100
head. Since all were dead whose dissatisfaction could injure
him, he was able to entrench himself with new measures,
civil and military, so that within the time of one year of
rule he was not only assured of Fermo but had become
formidable in the eyes of all his neighbors. It would have
been as difficult to oust him as Agathocles had he not let
himself be deceived by Cesare Borgia. For he was taken
with the Orsini and the Vitelli on the occasion referred to
above just a year after the parricide we have described and
was strangled along with Vitellozzo, who had been his 110
master in daring and crime.

Some may wonder how it could be that Agathocles and
his kind after countless acts of treachery and cruelty could
live very long secure in their fatherland and be able to
defend themselves against outside enemies with no conspiracies against them among their own citizens, inasmuch
as many others have failed because of their cruelty to preserve their state even in peaceful times, to say nothing of
the doubtful times of war. I believe that this depends on
whether cruelty is used well or ill. It may be said to be well 120
used (if we may speak of using well a thing in itself bad)

when all cruel deeds are committed at once in order to make sure of the state and thereafter discontinued to make way for the consideration of the welfare of the subjects. Bad use of cruelty we find in those cases where the cruel acts, though few to begin with, become more numerous with time. Those who practice the first kind may find some defense for their state in the eyes of God and man, but, as for the second class, it is impossible for them to stay in
130 power. Whence it is to be noted that a prince occupying a new state should see to it that he commit all his acts of cruelty at once so as not to be obliged to return to them every day, and thus, by abstaining from repeating them, he will be able to make men feel secure and can win them over by benefits. Whoever does otherwise, either through timidity or bad advice, is always obliged to go armed nor can he ever rely on his subjects since the latter, in view of continual fresh injuries, cannot feel safe with him. For injuries should be committed all at once so that, there being
140 less time to feel them, they give less offense, and favors should be dealt out a few at a time so that their effect may be more enduring. And above all a prince should live in a relationship to his subjects that does not have to be varied by any passing circumstance, good or evil, for in adversity harsh remedies are too late and the good that you may do is of no avail since it is counted as forced and you get no thanks for it.

# Chapter IX

## CIVIL MONARCHY

But to turn now to the other type whereby a citizen, not through villainy or intolerable violence, but by the favor of his fellow citizens, becomes Prince of a country; this can be called civil principality and it is not attained either wholly through ability or wholly through fortune but rather through shrewdness assisted by luck. To this kind of eminence one may ascend either by the will of the people or the favor of the great. For in every city there are these two different humors which have their origin in the desire
10 of the people to be free of the orders and oppression of the

great and the desire of the latter to order about and oppress the people. And from these two different urges comes one of three results in the city: either a one-man rule or liberty or anarchy. The rule of one is brought about either by the people or the great according as either one has the opportunity. For when the nobles see that they cannot resist the people they build up one of their own and make him prince in order to satisfy their ambitions under his protection. Or it may be that the people, unable to resist the nobles, will pick one man and make him prince so as to be protected by his authority. The one coming into power with the aid of the great finds it more difficult to maintain himself, for he is a ruler surrounded by many who think themselves his peers so that he cannot manipulate or command them as he would like to. He who comes to power by the favor of the people, however, finds himself alone in his eminence and has about him, at worst, only very few unprepared to obey him. Besides, one cannot fairly satisfy the great without injury to others, but that is not true of the people, whose objectives are more honest. For the former wish to exercise oppression, and the latter merely to avoid it. And it may be added too, that the prince can never feel safe from a hostile people since they are so many, but he can protect himself against the nobles, who are few. The worst a prince can fear from the people is that they will desert him, but from hostile nobles he may fear not only desertion but even their rising against him, for inasmuch as they are more far-seeing and sharp, they are always thinking ahead to protect themselves and looking for advantages on what they think will be the winning side. Then too the prince has to live always with the same people but he can well dispense with individual nobles since he can degrade them or create new ones every day and bestow honors or take them away at his pleasure.

To illustrate this part somewhat, I shall say that the privileged class may be one of two sorts: either they conduct themselves in such a way as to be under your obligation or not. Those who are, and are not rapacious, must be honored and cherished. Those who are not so bound to you may be of two sorts: either they act as they do out of pusillanimity or natural lack of spirit and in such cases you must use them, especially such as are of good counsel, since in prosperity they do you honor and in adversity you have nought to fear from them; but when they are of the second kind and deliberately refuse to be dependent on you, for their own scheming and ambitious reasons then you may be sure they are thinking more of themselves than you, and a prince should be very wary of such and regard them as open enemies, for in adversity they will always assist in 60 his ruin.

Hence one who attains power by favor of the people must keep the people always friendly to him, which will indeed be a simple matter, since all they ask is not to be oppressed; but one who, against the people, becomes a prince by favor of the nobles, must above all seek to win the friendship of the people, which will also be easy if he extends his protection to them. And since men, when they receive good from whence they expect evil, feel the more indebted to their benefactor, the people of such a prince 70 will be even more favorable to him than if he had attained his eminence by their favor. And the prince can win them over in many ways, which, as they vary according to the subject, need not be discussed here. I will sum up simply by saying that a prince must have a friendly people; otherwise he has nowhere to turn in adversity.

Nabis, Prince of the Spartans, sustained a siege by all Greece and a Roman army crowned with victories and successfully defended his fatherland against them. And it was enough, when danger drew near, for him to make sure of 80 very few, whereas had he had the people against him this would not have sufficed. And let no one refute my conclusion with the trite proverb "He who builds on the people builds on sand." That is true when a private citizen counts on the people and believes that they will free him if he should be oppressed by his enemies or by the magistrates; in this case a man may well be often deceived like the Gracchi in Rome and Giorgio Scali in Florence.[1] But if he who builds on the people be a prince and a man of courage, knowing how to command and not easily cast down by 90 adversities, and if he will make other necessary preparations and keep the general hope alive by his spirit and his measures, he will not be deceived by the people and will have reason to find his foundation well laid.

Regimes of this sort generally find their dangerous mo-

1. Leader of the people, abandoned by his followers and killed (1381).

ment when they are passing from the state of civil organization to absolutism. For the princes command either directly or through magistrates and in the latter case their position is weaker and more dangerous, for they are in the hands of the citizens appointed as magistrates who, especially in adversity, can easily take the state from them 100 either by opposing them or disobeying them. In time of danger too, the prince is not in a position to seize absolute authority, for the subjects and citizens, accustomed to receiving their orders from the magistrates, are not, in emergencies, disposed to accept his, and in critical times he will always have few in whom he can trust. Such a prince cannot count on what he sees in quiet times when the citizens have need of the state; at such times everyone runs to serve him, and everyone is lavish with promises; all are willing to die for him when death is far away, but in crucial days, 110 when the state needs its citizens, then few are to be found. This experience is the more critical as it is to be suffered but once. Hence a wise prince must adopt a policy which will insure that his citizens always and in all circumstances will have need of his government; then they will always be faithful to him.

# Chapter X

## HOW THE STRENGTH OF ALL MONARCHIES SHOULD BE MEASURED

In examining the characteristics of this kind of regime, there is another consideration to be taken into account: which is whether a prince has a state of such resources as will enable him to stand on his own feet in case of need or whether he must always have the assistance of others. To make the point a little clearer, I mean by those who can stand on their own feet such princes as are able, through abundance of men or money, to build up an adequate army and take the field against anyone likely to attack them, and I call dependent on others such as are not 10 strong enough to appear against the enemy in the field but must rather retire behind their walls and seek their protection therein. We have touched on the first category and later we shall say all that is necessary concerning them.

As for the second, there is little to say save to encourage such princes to supply and fortify their own cities and ignore the outlying land. Whoever has his cities well fortified and has acted toward his subjects along lines indicated above (and to be further set forth later) will find that his attacker will think twice, for men are hesitant about enterprises which seem likely to present difficulties, and it will be clearly apparent that one who has his cities in good shape for defense and is not hated by his people will not be an enemy easy to overcome. The cities of Germany enjoy the greatest freedom; they have little territory outside the walls and they obey the emperor when they will, fearing neither him nor any other powerful lord in their vicinity, for they are so well fortified that everyone realizes it would be a laborious and difficult matter to take them. They all have moats and walls of adequate measure, sufficient artillery, and in their public reserves enough food, drink, and fuel for a year. Further, in order to keep the working people satisfied and to see that the public does not suffer, they have always enough resources to provide work for a year in such skills as form the life and fibre of the city and in crafts whereby the workers gain their livelihood. They have high regard for military exercises and have provided the necessary measures for maintaining them. So a prince who holds a really strong city and is not hated by the people cannot be attacked, and, if by chance he were, his assailant would have to abandon the enterprise in discredit, for circumstances are so changeable that it is almost impossible to keep a besieging army encamped during a year of idleness.

It may be said that if the people have possessions outside the walls and are compelled to stand by and see them burned they will lose patience, and the long siege and their own self-interest will make them forget their obligation to the prince. But my answer is that a powerful and spirited prince will always overcome such difficulties, giving his people to hope that the ill cannot long endure, playing on their fear of the enemy's cruelty and knowing how to protect himself against those who are too outspoken. It is further to be expected that the enemy will burn and ravage the land as soon as he begins the siege, while the spirits of

the defenders are still high and enthusiastic; thus the prince
will have less to fear, for later, when spirits are somewhat
cooled, the damage has already been done, the evils have
been suffered, and there is no further hope; then the people
will draw even closer to their prince, holding him under  60
obligation to them as their houses have been burned and
their property ravaged in his defense. It is in the nature of
men to see obligation in the favors they have conferred
just as in the benefits they have received. Hence if the matter be well considered we shall see that early and late in
the siege a prudent prince will not find it difficult to keep
his citizens steadfast in spirit if only they do not lack food
and material for defense.

# Chapter XI

## ECCLESIASTICAL MONARCHIES

We have now left to consider only ecclesiastical states;
in their case all the difficulties come before possession, for
they are acquired either through ability or fortune and can
be maintained without either. For they are supported by
time-honored laws of religion, so powerful and of such
nature as to leave their princes always in authority whatever kind of policy they may follow or whatever sort of life
they may lead. Such princes alone have states and do not
defend them, and subjects and do not govern them, and
their states though undefended are not taken from them.  10
Their subjects make no complaint though ungoverned and
neither have the will nor the power to break away from
them. These then are the only safe and happy principalities. Since, however, they are under the guidance of a
higher influence beyond the grasp of the human mind, I
will say nothing of them. Set up and maintained by God, as
they are, it would be the act of a rash and presumptuous
man to analyze them.

However, if I am asked how it is that the present temporal power of the Church has become so great—for before  20
Alexander the Italian potentates, and not only they but
every petty baron and lord had little respect for it, while

now it can frighten a king of France and drive him from
Italy and ruin the Venetians—although the causes may be
known well enough, it will not seem to me out of place to
refer to them here.

Before Charles of France came into Italy the peninsula
was ruled by five powers: the Pope, the Venetians, the
King of Naples, the Duke of Milan, and the Florentines.
30 These rulers had to keep two objects in mind: one, that a
foreigner should not be allowed to enter Italy, the other,
that no one of the five should increase his domain. Those
who gave most concern were the Pope and the Venetians.
To keep the Venetians in check it took a union of all the
others, as on the occasion of the defense of Ferrara.[1] To
keep the Pope down the barons of Rome were employed.
These were divided in two factions: the Orsini and the
Colonna, and hence there was always a motive for brawl-
ing between them and, being armed and placed as they
40 were very close to the Pope, they kept the Papacy weak and
powerless. And even though a vigorous Pope might arise,
like Sixtus,[2] yet neither fortune nor wisdom could free him
from these inconveniences. The reason lay in the shortness
of a Pope's life for, in the ten years which was the average
rule of a Pope, he could only with difficulty break down one
of these factions, and if, for example, one had almost succeeded in crushing the Colonna, a new Pope would come
in hostile to the Orsini and he would raise up the former
faction and would not have time to crush the other.

50 This caused the temporal power of the Pope to be held in
little esteem in Italy. Then came Alexander VI. More
than any other Pontiff we have ever had, he showed the
extent to which a Pope's power could prevail through
money and force. With Valentino as his agent and the
coming of the French as the occasion, he accomplished all
the things I have listed above when discussing the actions
of the Duke. And although he did not aim so much at
the aggrandizement of the Church, as of the Duke, nonetheless the result of his activities was to increase the power
60 of the Church, which at his death, the Duke out of the

1. In 1482 a coalition of the Papacy, the Kingdom of Naples,
Milan, and Florence was formed to drive the Venetians from Fer-
rarese territory.
2. Sixtus IV, Francesco della Rovere (1414-1484, proclaimed
Pope in 1471).

way, was the beneficiary of his labors. Then came Pope Julius and found the Church powerful and in possession of all Romagna. The barons of Rome had been crushed, and the two factions rendered harmless by the blows of Alexander. Julius also found ways at hand to accumulate money, never made use of before Alexander. The former not only followed the policies of his predecessor but went further and planned to win Bologna, crush the Venetians, and drive the French from Italy. In all he was successful and with the greater honor to him as he did everything to 70 further the power of the Church and not an individual. He kept the Orsini and Colonna factions in the condition in which he found them, and though there have been leaders among them apt to revolt, yet two things have kept them quiet: one, the greatness of the Church, which dismayed them, and the other, the fact that they had no cardinals. These prelates are the source of their dissensions, nor will the factions ever be quiet whenever they have cardinals, since these foment partisan strife in Rome and outside, and the barons are constrained to defend their factions; 80 thus from the ambition of the prelates arise the discords and turmoils of the barons. His Holiness Pope Leo [3] has thus found the present pontificate in a very strong position, whence we may hope that as his predecessors have made it powerful by force of arms, he will make it great and venerable by his kindness and infinite other virtues.

# Chapter XII

## VARIOUS KINDS OF TROOPS WITH SPECIAL DISCUSSION OF MERCENARIES

I have now discussed in detail all the characteristics of such monarchies as in the beginning I had set out to analyze, and have given some consideration to the causes of their success or failure, showing as well in what ways many have attempted to acquire them. I have now to speak in a more general way of offensive and defensive measures

3. Leo X, Giovanni de' Medici. (1475-1521) See Introduction.

which may be used in each of the above mentioned principalities.

We have said above that a Prince must have strong foundations, otherwise his downfall is inevitable. The main
foundations of all states, new, old, or mixed, are good laws
and good arms; and since there cannot be good laws where
there are not good arms and likewise where there are good
arms the laws must be good too, I shall omit discussion of
laws and speak only of arms. Now the arms with which
a Prince defends his state are either his own, or mercenary,
or auxiliary, or mixed. Mercenaries and auxiliaries are useless and dangerous, and a leader having his state built on
mercenary armies will never be secure. Troops of this
sort are disunited, ambitious, undisciplined, and faithless,
swaggering when among friends and cowardly in the face
of the enemy; they have neither fear of God nor loyalty to
men. Ruin is postponed only as long as the assault is postponed; in times of peace you are despoiled by them and in
time of war by the enemy. The reason is that they have
no other interest or incentive to hold the field, save only
their moderate pay, which is not enough to make them
willing to die for you. They are pleased to be your soldiers
so long as you have no war; when it comes they either run
away or leave your employ. It should not be hard to persuade the reader of the truth of this, for the ruin of Italy
springs from no other cause than this error of having placed
confidence over so many years in mercenary troops. Some
individuals indeed profited by them, and they seemed bold
enough when they had each other to fight, but when the
foreigner came in they showed their true colors. Hence it
came about that Charles of France was able to take Italy
"with chalk" [1] and those who said it was because of our sins
were speaking the truth, but it was the sins I have mentioned and not others that may have been meant. And
since the sins were the sins of Princes they have paid the
penalty too.

I shall try to show more clearly the disadvantages of this
kind of troops. Mercenary leaders are either excellent men
or they are not. If they are, then you cannot trust them for
they will always have their own aspirations to power and
so will either attack you, their master, or oppress others

1. i.e., by merely marking with chalk the quarters to be allotted
to his soldiers.

beyond your purposes. And if the leader be not a man of
ability then you are generally sure to be ruined by him. If
the objection is made that any armed leader, mercenary or 50
not, will do the same, I will answer by saying how arms
should be used either by a prince or a republic. The Prince
must go in person to act as captain, and the republic must
send its own citizens. If the man chosen turns out to be
worthless, he must be removed, and if he is efficient he
must be kept in check by the necessary measures. Experience has shown us that princes using their own forces and
armed republics achieve great success, but mercenary arms
do only harm. An army of citizens is more loath to accept
the dictatorship of one of its leaders than an army of for- 60
eign mercenaries. Rome and Sparta lived armed and free
through many centuries. The Swiss are heavily armed and
have the greatest freedom.

For the use of mercenaries in antiquity we may cite the
case of the Carthaginians, who were almost conquered by
their own hired soldiery after the first war with the Romans, even though the leaders were Carthaginian citizens.
Philip of Macedon was made leader of the Thebans on the
death of Epaminondas and after winning the victory he deprived them of liberty. The Milanese on the death of Duke 70
Philip,[2] employed Francesco Sforza against the Venetians,
and after he had overcome the enemy at Caravaggio[3] he
combined with them to turn on his masters. His father, the
elder Sforza,[4] employed by Queen Giovanna of Naples,
without warning left her defenseless so that to preserve her
kingdom she was compelled to appeal to the King of
Aragon for protection. And if the Venetians and the Florentines have in the past added to their empires by this
kind of arms and have had their captains defend them
without making themselves princes the answer is, as re- 80
gards the Florentines, they have been very lucky. For of
the good captains who might have given them cause to
fear, some have not been victorious, some have had rivals,
and others have turned their ambitions elsewhere. The one
who was not victorious was Giovanni Acuto[5] and since he

2. Filippo Maria, last of the Visconti, died in 1447.    3. In 1448.
4. Muzio Attendolo, nicknamed Sforza (1369-1424).
5. Italianized form of John Hawkwood (1320?-1394). Knighted
by Edward III for his services in the French wars, he assembled a
body of mercenaries known as the "White Company" and went into
Italy.

had no victory there is no way of knowing how loyal he might have been, but everyone will admit that if he had won, the Florentines would have been at his mercy. Sforza had always the Braccio [6] clique as rivals and they kept an eye on each other. Francesco turned his ambition to Lombardy and Braccio to the Church and the Kingdom of Naples.

But let us look at recent events. The Florentines made Paolo Vitelli [7] their captain, a most intelligent man, who starting from private station had acquired great renown. Had he taken Pisa, no one will deny that the Florentines would have had to keep him (for if he had passed over to their enemies there would have been no hope for them) and keeping him, they would have had to obey him.

If we look at the rise of the Venetians, we shall see that their actions were wise and glorious so long as they carried on wars with their own troops. Before they turned to their land campaigns they carried out valorous operations with their own gentlemen and armed people, but when they took up their land enterprises they gave up this laudable practice and followed the customs of Italy. And in the beginnings of their expansion on land, since they had no great holdings and their prestige was high, they had little to fear from their captains, but as their acquisitions increased, which was under Carmagnola, [8] they had an indication of their mistaken policy. Finding him a man of valor and ability, whose leadership had brought them victory over the Duke of Milan, and yet learning, on the other hand, that he was lukewarm in his conduct of the war, they decided that they could no longer win under his command and they would not and could not dismiss him else they would have lost all they had won. So, in order to assure their safety, they were obliged to kill him. Since then they have had as captains Bartolommeo da Bergamo, [9] Roberto

90

100

110

6. Braccio da Montone (1368-1424) at one time master of Umbria and a large part of the Marche.

7. Suspected of treason and executed by the Florentines in 1499. His brother, Vitellozzo, was one of the captains strangled by order of Cesare Borgia at Sinigaglia (1502). The family included other celebrated *condottieri*.

8. Francesco Bussone, Conte di Carmagnola (1390?-1432). Fought first for Filippo Visconti, later for the Venetians.

9. Known as Colleoni (died 1475). Verrocchio's statue of him is one of the artistic treasures of Venice

da San Severino,[10] the Count of Pitigliano,[11] and the like, 120
with whom they had to fear losses rather than gains. Indeed they learned as much at Vailà [12] where in one day
they lost all that 800 years of effort had won for them. From
this kind of arms come only slow, late, and unstable acquisitions, and sudden and miraculous losses.

As I have arrived at Italian cases in my references, I
should like to go back a little—for Italy has been governed
by such arms for many years now—and examine the ori-
gins and development of this kind of warfare so that it
may be more easily corrected. You must know that in the 130
recent past, as Italy began to shake loose from the Empire,
and the temporal power of the Pope began to be held in
more esteem, the country was divided into several states.
For many great cities took up arms against their nobles,
who had previously, under the authority of the Empire,
held them in subjection; the Church favored such move-
ments in order to increase her temporal prestige, and in
many cities individual citizens made themselves princes. In
this way all Italy came under the rule either of the Church
or some republic, and, as neither priests nor ordinary burgh- 140
ers were familiar with the use of arms, they began to use
foreign mercenary troops. The first leader to bring this
kind of soldiery into prominence was Alberigo da Conio,[13]
of Romagna. Among his pupils were Braccio and Sforza,
who in their day were arbiters of Italy. Then came all the
others who up to our time have directed all the troops in
Italy, and the result of their valor and skill has been that
the country has been overrun by Charles, sacked by Louis,
violated by Ferdinand, and held in contempt by the Swiss.

Their policy has been, first of all, to deprecate the infan- 150
try in order to exalt their own troops. This they did because
they had no land and lived on their earnings, and so a small
body of infantry could not add to their prestige, and a large
body would have been too much for them to support. So
they limited themselves to horse, of which a tolerable
number would yield them honor and sustenance. Things
reached such a point that you would scarcely find two
thousand infantry in an army of twenty thousand. Further

10. Died 1487.
11. Niccolò Orsini (1442-1510).
12. In 1509 they were defeated at Vailà by Julius II and his allies.
13. Alberigo da Barbiano, Conte di Conio (died 1409).

it was a main part of their policy to do away with any possible cause of hardship or danger; there was no killing in their skirmishes but only the taking of prisoners without expectation of ransom. There were no night attacks on fortified positions nor were there night sallies from such positions against the bivouacs; no ditches or stockades were built around the camps, and there was no campaigning in winter. Such things were permissible in their military code and indeed devised by them, as we have said, in order to spare themselves hardship and risk. In this manner they have reduced Italy to a state of servitude and made her an object of contempt.

# Chapter XIII

## AUXILIARIES, MIXED, AND NATIVE TROOPS

By auxiliary arms—which are the other kind of useless arms—are meant the arms of a powerful foreigner whom you invite to assist you in your defense. The action of Pope Julius is a recent example; having seen at Ferrara [1] the sorry proof of his mercenaries, he turned to auxiliaries and made an agreement with Ferdinand of Spain by which the latter was to aid him with his armies. Such troops may be good or bad in themselves but they are always harmful to the one who makes use of them. If you lose with them you are undone; if you win you become their prisoner. Ancient history is full of examples, but I do not wish to put aside the case of Pope Julius, so fresh in our memories. His decision could hardly have been less well-founded, for in his eagerness for Ferrara he put himself entirely in the hands of a foreigner. Only a third factor, brought about by his good fortune, saved him from reaping the fruit of his bad decision. For when his auxiliaries were beaten at Ravenna the Swiss arose and drove out the victors, much to his and others' surprise; thus he escaped being made a prisoner by his enemies, who were put to flight, or by his own auxiliaries, as he had won with other arms than theirs. The Florentines, being completely unarmed, brought ten thousand

1. In 1510.

French to assault Pisa and this action of theirs was more dangerous to them than any crisis in their tumultuous history.

The emperor of Constantinople[2] to rid himself of his enemies, brought into Greece an army of ten thousand Turks, who refused to leave when the war was over; this was the beginning of the enslavement of Greece by the infidel.

If any one, therefore, wants to make sure of not winning he will avail himself of troops such as these. They are much more dangerous than mercenaries, for under their service your downfall is assured, as they are all united and all under the command of another, but the mercenaries, when they have secured a victory, must await the time and the occasion to do you harm as they are under different captains and all in your pay, hence a third party you may designate as head cannot immediately assume such authority as to injure you. In short, in mercenaries cowardice and unwillingness to fight are what you have most to fear, but in auxiliaries it is rather their valor and effectiveness. Hence a wise prince has always avoided use of arms of this sort and has rather depended on his own, being willing to lose with the latter rather than win with the former and correctly judging that victories won by others are not really victories.

I am never loath to cite Cesare Borgia and his actions. This Duke entered Romagna with auxiliary arms, as his troops were all French, and with their aid occupied Imola and Forlì, but when it seemed to him that such troops were not to be trusted he turned to the mercenaries as being less dangerous and took Vitelli and the Orsini into his pay; finding these difficult, untrustworthy, and dangerous to direct, he then did away with them and relied on troops of his own. Here we may easily see the differences between these various kinds of arms, in the light of the differences in the phases of the Duke's prestige when he had French troops and when he had the Orsini and the Vitelli and when he was left with his own soldiers and dependent on himself. His authority increased with these successive changes, nor was he ever so highly esteemed, as when all knew that he was the complete master of his own troops.

2. John Cantacuzene in 1353.

I do not wish to leave these fresh Italian examples, but I cannot omit Hiero of Syracuse, whom I have mentioned before. When the Syracusans made this man head of their armies, he realized immediately that the mercenary militia was useless, as the leaders were of the same stamp as our recent *condottieri,* and since he could not see his way either to keep them nor to abandon them, he had them cut in pieces, after which he waged war with his own troops and not with those of others. I wish also to take note of a figure of the Old Testament which is to our purpose here. When David volunteered before Saul to go forth to battle with Goliath, the Philistine challenger, Saul, in order to encourage David, armed him with his own arms, but when the latter tried them on he refused to wear them, saying that in those arms he could not give a good account of himself and preferred to encounter the enemy with his own knife and sling. In short, another's arms will either fall from your back or weigh you down or bind you. Charles VII,[3] father of King Louis XI, having by his fortune and valor liberated France from the English, realized the necessity of arming himself with his own arms and set up in his kingdom measures for organizing men-at-arms and infantry. Later, King Louis, his son, dispensed with the infantry and began to employ the Swiss, and this mistake brought others in its train, and was, as the facts now show us, the cause of the present dangers of that kingdom. Having built up the reputation of the Swiss, he has debased his own arms, for he has completely done away with the infantry, and he has made his cavalry dependent on the support of others, for since they have become accustomed to operations supported by the Swiss, they have come to believe that they cannot win without them. Hence it comes about that the French alone cannot stand up to the Swiss, and without the Swiss they cannot withstand others. The armies of France, therefore, have been mixed, partly mercenaries and partly her own. Such troops, taken together, are much better than mercenaries or auxiliaries alone, but very inferior to one's own armies.

The examples given may suffice, for the Kingdom of France would be invincible if the ordinances of Charles had been strengthened or maintained, but the short-sight-

---

3. 1403-1461, crowned 1429. Joan of Arc's king.

edness of man is pleased with innovations that bring immediate advantage, and overlooks the slow working poison underneath, as I said above of hectic fevers. On this account, if one who rules a state does not recognize ills before they come into existence, he is not really wise, and this is given to few. And if we consider the first downfall of the Roman Empire we shall find that it had its beginning simply in the hiring of Goths, and from that beginning the strength of the Roman Empire began to grow weak, and all the valor that was taken from it was transferred to them.

My conclusion, therefore, is that no state is safe unless it has its own arms, rather it is completely dependent on fortune, having no effectiveness to defend itself in adversity. It was always the opinion and the observation of wise men that there is nothing so inferior or unstable as the reputation of power not founded on its own strength. Your own arms are those composed of your subjects or citizens or dependents, all others are either mercenaries or auxiliaries. The way to organize one's own arms will be easily found if the measures indicated above are studied, and if one observes how Philip, the father of Alexander the Great, and many republics and princes have organized their arms. To such principles I leave the reader without further comment.

# Chapter XIV

## THE PRINCE'S DUTY IN MILITARY MATTERS

The principal study and care and the especial profession of a prince should be warfare and its attendant rules and discipline. This is the only art pertaining to him who commands, and it is an art of such value that not only does it preserve those who were born princes, but often enables men of private station to reach that rank; and conversely we can see that when princes have given more thought to the amenities than to arms they have lost their states. The basic cause of such a loss is neglect of this art, and the main cause of winning a state is to be expert on this score.

Francesco Sforza, because of his skill in arms, rose from private station to be Duke of Milan, and his sons, who avoided the hardships and discomforts of bearing arms, have fallen from the rank of Duke back to private station. For, in addition to other ills, being unarmed makes you an object of contempt, which is one of those infamies against which a prince must guard himself, as we shall see later. Between an armed man and an unarmed man there is no comparison whatever, and it is not reasonable to expect that one who is armed will be happy to obey one without arms, nor that the latter will feel secure in being guarded by armed servants. Since one is bound to feel contempt and the other suspicion, it is not possible for them to work together. So that a prince who has no understanding of military affairs, in addition to his other woes as aforementioned, cannot be held in esteem by his soldiers and cannot have confidence in them.

Hence he must never let his mind be turned from the study of warfare and in times of peace he must concern himself with it more than in those of war; this he can do in two ways—with acts and with thought. As for his actions, in addition to having his troops well-organized and well-trained, he should be fond of hunting and thereby accustom his body to hardships, learning, at the same time, the nature of topography, how mountains slope, how they are cut by valleys, how the plains lie, and the nature of rivers and swamps. And he should give great care to these matters, for such knowledge has two uses: first, he learns to know his own country and can the better understand its defenses; second, through the knowledge and experience of his own country, he can more easily understand other regions when the necessity arises; for the hills, valleys, plains, and swamps of, let us say, Tuscany have a certain resemblance to such features of other provinces, so so that from knowledge of the topography of one province one can easily attain to a knowledge of the nature of others. A prince who does not have this skill lacks the first essential of a good leader. For it is in this way that you learn how to come upon the enemy, secure camping sites, lead armies, prepare battles, and plan sieges to your advantage.

Among the other favorable comments historians have to make concerning Philipoemen, Prince of the Achaeans, is that in times of peace he never thought of anything but the ways of waging war. When he was riding in the country with his friends he would often stop and consult with them, asking: If the enemy were on that hill and we were here with our armies, which of us would have the more advantageous position? And how would we go about in safety and keeping our ranks? If we wished to withdraw how would we do so? And how would we pursue them if they were to retreat? And he would set before them, as they rode along, all possible cases that might occur on a campaign; he would hear their opinion and express his own, supporting it with his reasons. Thus because of these continual cogitations it was impossible that any accident could arise, if he were leading an army, for which he would not have a remedy prepared.

As for the exercise of the mind, the prince should read the histories of all peoples and ponder on the actions of the wise men therein recorded, note how they governed themselves in time of war, examine the reasons for their victories or defeats in order to imitate the former and avoid the latter, and above all conduct himself in accordance with the example of some great man of the past who took as a model a praiseworthy and glorious predecessor, whose actions and attitudes he has had always before him, as they say Alexander the Great imitated Achilles, Caesar, Alexander, and Scipio, Cyrus. Whoever reads the life of the aforesaid Cyrus written by Xenophon must recognize in the life of Scipio how much such imitation was the source of his glory and how closely in chastity, affability, humanity, and liberality Scipio conformed to those things Xenophon had written of Cyrus. A wise prince must observe such manners as these and never be idle in times of peace but rather by his industry make capital of them, as it were, for use in adversity so that when fortune turns against him he will be prepared to resist her blows.

# Chapter XV

## ON THINGS FOR WHICH MEN, AND PARTICULARLY PRINCES, ARE PRAISED OR BLAMED

We now have left to consider what should be the manners and attitudes of a prince toward his subjects and his friends. As I know that many have written on this subject I feel that I may be held presumptuous in what I have to say, if in my comments I do not follow the lines laid down by others. Since, however, it has been my intention to write something which may be of use to the understanding reader, it has seemed wiser to me to follow the real truth of the matter rather than what we imagine it to be. For imagination has created many principalities and republics that have never been seen or known to have any real existence, for how we live is so different from how we ought to live that he who studies what ought to be done rather than what is done will learn the way to his downfall rather than to his preservation. A man striving in every way to be good will meet his ruin among the great number who are not good. Hence it is necessary for a prince, if he wishes to remain in power, to learn how not to be good and to use his knowledge or refrain from using it as he may need.

Putting aside then the things imagined as pertaining to a prince and considering those that really do, I will say that all men, and particularly princes because of their prominence, when comment is made of them, are noted as having some characteristics deserving either praise or blame. One is accounted liberal, another stingy, to use a Tuscan term—for in our speech avaricious (*avaro*) is applied to such as are desirous of acquiring by rapine whereas stingy (*misero*) is the term used for those who are reluctant to part with their own—one is considered bountiful, another rapacious; one cruel, another tenderhearted; one false to his word, another trustworthy; one effeminate and pusillanimous, another wild and spirited; one humane, another haughty; one lascivious, another chaste; one a man of integrity and another sly; one tough and another pliant; one serious and another frivolous; one religious and another skeptical, and so on. Everyone will agree, I know, that it would be a most praiseworthy thing if all the qualities accounted as good in the above enumeration were found in a Prince. But since they cannot be so possessed nor observed because of human conditions which do not allow of it, what is necessary for the prince is to be prudent enough to escape the infamy of such vices as would result in the loss of his state; as for the others which would not have that effect, he must guard himself from them as far as possible but if he cannot, he may overlook them as being of less importance. Further, he should have no concern about incurring the infamy of such vices without which the preservation of his state would be difficult. For, if the matter be well considered, it will be seen that some habits which appear virtuous, if adopted would signify ruin, and others that seem vices lead to security and the well-being of the prince.

# Chapter XVI

## GENEROSITY AND MEANNESS

To begin then with the first characteristic set forth above, I will say that it would be well always to be considered generous, yet generosity used in such a way as not to bring you honor does you harm, for if it is practiced virtuously and as it is meant to be practiced it will not be publicly known and you will not lose the name of being just the opposite of generous. Hence to preserve the reputation of being generous among your friends you must not neglect any kind of lavish display, yet a prince of this sort will consume all his property in such gestures and, if he wishes to preserve his reputation for generosity, he will be forced to levy heavy taxes on his subjects and turn to fiscal measures and do everything possible to get money. Thus he will begin to be regarded with hatred by his subjects and should he become poor he will be held in scant esteem; having by his prodigality given offense to many and rewarded only a few, he will suffer at the first hint of adversity, and the first

danger will be critical for him. Yet when he realizes this and tries to reform he will immediately get the name of
20 being a miser. So a prince, as he is unable to adopt the virtue of generosity without danger to himself, must, if he is a wise man, accept with indifference the name of miser. For with the passage of time he will be regarded as increasingly generous when it is seen that, by virtue of his parsimony, his income suffices for him to defend himself in wartime and undertake his enterprises without heavily taxing his people. For in that way he practices generosity towards all from whom he refrains from taking money, who are many, and stinginess only toward those from
30 whom he withholds gifts, who are few.

In our times we have seen great things accomplished only by such as have had the name of misers; all others have come to naught. Pope Julius made use of his reputation for generosity to make himself Pope but later, in order to carry on his war against the King of France, he made no effort to maintain it; and he has waged a great number of wars without having had recourse to heavy taxation because his persistent parsimony has made up for the extra expenses. The present King of Spain, had he had
40 any reputation for generosity, would never have carried through to victory so many enterprises.

A prince then, if he wishes not to rob his subjects but to be able to defend himself and not to become poor and despised nor to be obliged to become rapacious, must consider it a matter of small importance to incur the name of miser, for this is one of the vices which keep him on his throne. Some may say Caesar through generosity won his way to the purple, and others either through being generous or being accounted so have risen to the highest ranks.
50 But I will answer by pointing out that either you are already a prince or you are on the way to becoming one and in the first case generosity is harmful while in the second it is very necessary to be considered open-handed. Caesar was seeking to arrive at the domination of Rome but if he had survived after reaching his goal and had not moderated his lavishness he would certainly have destroyed the empire.

It might also be objected that there have been many princes, accomplishing great things with their armies, who
60 have been acclaimed for their generosity. To which I

would answer that the prince either spends his own (or his subjects') money or that of others; in the first case he must be very sparing but in the second he should overlook no aspect of open-handedness. So the prince who leads his armies and lives on looting and extortion and booty, thus handling the wealth of others, must indeed have this quality of generosity for otherwise his soldiers will not follow him. You can be very free with wealth not belonging to yourself or your subjects, in the fashion of Cyrus, Caesar, or Alexander, for spending what belongs to others rather 70 enhances your reputation than detracts from it; it is only spending your own wealth that is dangerous. There is nothing that consumes itself as does prodigality; even as you practice it you lose the faculty of practicing it and either you become poor and despicable or, in order to escape poverty, rapacious and unpopular. And among the things a prince must guard against is precisely the danger of becoming an object either of contempt or of hatred. Generosity leads you to both these evils, wherefore it is wiser to accept the name of miserly, since the reproach it 80 brings is without hatred, than to seek a reputation for generosity and thus perforce acquire the name of rapacious, which breeds hatred as well as infamy.

# Chapter XVII

## CRUELTY AND CLEMENCY AND WHETHER IT IS BETTER TO BE LOVED OR FEARED

Now to continue with the list of characteristics. It should be the desire of every prince to be considered merciful and not cruel, yet he should take care not to make poor use of his clemency. Cesare Borgia was regarded as cruel, yet his cruelty reorganized Romagna and united it in peace and loyalty. Indeed, if we reflect, we shall see that this man was more merciful than the Florentines who, to avoid the charge of cruelty, allowed Pistoia to be destroyed.[1] A prince should care nothing for the accusation of cruelty so long as he keeps his subjects united and loyal; by making 10

1. By unchecked rioting between opposing factions (1502).

a very few examples he can be more truly merciful than those who through too much tender-heartedness allow disorders to arise whence come killings and rapine. For these offend an entire community, while the few executions ordered by the prince affect only a few individuals. For a new prince above all it is impossible not to earn a reputation for cruelty since new states are full of dangers. Virgil indeed has Dido apologize for the inhumanity of her rule because it is new, in the words:

20
> Res dura et regni novitas me talia cogunt
> Moliri et late fines custode tueri.[2]

Nevertheless a prince should not be too ready to listen to talebearers nor to act on suspicion, nor should he allow himself to be easily frightened. He should proceed with a mixture of prudence and humanity in such a way as not to be made incautious by overconfidence nor yet intolerable by excessive mistrust.

Here the question arises; whether it is better to be loved than feared or feared than loved. The answer is that it 30 would be desirable to be both but, since that is difficult, it is much safer to be feared than to be loved, if one must choose. For on men in general this observation may be made: they are ungrateful, fickle, and deceitful, eager to avoid dangers, and avid for gain, and while you are useful to them they are all with you, offering you their blood, their property, their lives, and their sons so long as danger is remote, as we noted above, but when it approaches they turn on you. Any prince, trusting only in their words and having no other preparations made, will fall to his ruin, for 40 friendships that are bought at a price and not by greatness and nobility of soul are paid for indeed, but they are not owned and cannot be called upon in time of need. Men have less hesitation in offending a man who is loved than one who is feared, for love is held by a bond of obligation which, as men are wicked, is broken whenever personal advantage suggests it, but fear is accompanied by the dread of punishment which never relaxes.

Yet a prince should make himself feared in such a way that, if he does not thereby merit love, at least he may es-

2. . . . my cruel fate
And doubts attending an unsettled state
Force me to guard my coast from foreign foes. (Dryden)

cape odium, for being feared and not hated may well go to- 50
gether. And indeed the prince may attain this end if he but
respect the property and the women of his subjects and citizens. And if it should become necessary to seek the death
of someone, he should find a proper justification and a
public cause, and above all he should keep his hands off another's property, for men forget more readily the death of
their father than the loss of their patrimony. Besides, pretexts for seizing property are never lacking, and when a
prince begins to live by means of rapine he will always find
some excuse for plundering others, and conversely pretexts 60
for execution are rarer and are more quickly exhausted.

A prince at the head of his armies and with a vast number of soldiers under his command should give not the
slightest heed if he is esteemed cruel, for without such a
reputation he will not be able to keep his army united and
ready for action. Among the marvelous things told of Hannibal is that, having a vast army under his command made
up of all kinds and races of men and waging war far from
his own country, he never allowed any dissension to arise
either as between the troops and their leaders or among the 70
troops themselves, and this both in times of good fortune
and bad. This could only have come about through his
most inhuman cruelty which, taken in conjunction with
his great valor, kept him always an object of respect and
terror in the eyes of his soldiers. And without the cruelty
his other characteristics would not have achieved this
effect. Thoughtless writers have admired his actions and at
the same time deplored the cruelty which was the basis of
them. As evidence of the truth of our statement that his
other virtues would have been insufficient let us examine 80
the case of Scipio, an extraordinary leader not only in his
own day but for all recorded history. His army in Spain
revolted and for no other reason than because of his kind-
heartedness, which had allowed more license to his soldiery than military discipline properly permits. His policy
was attacked in the Senate by Fabius Maximus, who called
him a corrupter of the Roman arms. When the Locrians
had been mishandled by one of his lieutenants, his easy-
going nature prevented him from avenging them or disci-
plining his officer, and it was à propos of this incident that 90
one of the senators remarked, wishing to find an excuse
for him, that there were many men who knew better how

to avoid error themselves than to correct it in others. This characteristic of Scipio would have clouded his fame and glory had he continued in authority, but as he lived under the government of the Senate, its harmful aspect was hidden and it reflected credit on him.

Hence, on the subject of being loved or feared I will conclude that since love depends on the subjects, but the prince
100 has it in his own hands to create fear, a wise prince will rely on what is his own, remembering at the same time that he must avoid arousing hatred, as we have said.

# Chapter XVIII

## IN WHAT MANNER PRINCES SHOULD KEEP THEIR WORD

How laudable it is for a prince to keep his word and govern his actions by integrity rather than trickery will be understood by all. Nonetheless we have in our times seen great things accomplished by many princes who have thought little of keeping their promises and have known the art of mystifying the minds of men. Such princes have won out over those whose actions were based on fidelity to their word.

It must be understood that there are two ways of fight-
10 ing, one with laws and the other with arms. The first is the way of men, the second is the style of beasts, but since very often the first does not suffice it is necessary to turn to the second. Therefore a prince must know how to play the beast as well as the man. This lesson was taught allegorically by the ancient writers who related that Achilles and many other princes were brought up by Chiron the Centaur, who took them under his discipline. The clear significance of this half-man and half-beast preceptorship is that a prince must know how to use either of these two na-
20 tures and that one without the other has no enduring strength. Now since the prince must make use of the characteristics of beasts he should choose those of the fox and the lion, though the lion cannot defend himself against snares and the fox is helpless against wolves. One must be

a fox in avoiding traps and a lion in frightening wolves. Such as choose simply the rôle of a lion do not rightly understand the matter. Hence a wise leader cannot and should not keep his word when keeping it is not to his advantage or when the reasons that made him give it are no longer valid. If men were good, this would not be a good precept, but since they are wicked and will not keep faith with you, you are not bound to keep faith with them.

A prince has never lacked legitimate reasons to justify his breach of faith. We could give countless recent examples and show how any number of peace treaties or promises have been broken and rendered meaningless by the faithlessness of princes, and how success has fallen to the one who best knows how to counterfeit the fox. But it is necessary to know how to disguise this nature well and how to pretend and dissemble. Men are so simple and so ready to follow the needs of the moment that the deceiver will always find some one to deceive. Of recent examples I shall mention one. Alexander VI did nothing but deceive and never thought of anything else and always found some occasion for it. Never was there a man more convincing in his asseverations nor more willing to offer the most solemn oaths nor less likely to observe them. Yet his deceptions were always successful for he was an expert in this field.

So a prince need not have all the aforementioned good qualities, but it is most essential that he appear to have them. Indeed, I should go so far as to say that having them and always practising them is harmful, while seeming to have them is useful. It is good to appear clement, trustworthy, humane, religious, and honest, and also to be so, but always with the mind so disposed that, when the occasion arises not to be so, you can become the opposite. It must be understood that a prince and particularly a new prince cannot practise all the virtues for which men are accounted good, for the necessity of preserving the state often compels him to take actions which are opposed to loyalty, charity, humanity, and religion. Hence he must have a spirit ready to adapt itself as the varying winds of fortune command him. As I have said, so far as he is able, a prince should stick to the path of good but, if the necessity arises, he should know how to follow evil.

A prince must take great care that no word ever passes

his lips that is not full of the above mentioned five good qualities, and he must seem to all who see and hear him a
70 model of piety, loyalty, integrity, humanity, and religion. Nothing is more necessary than to seem to possess this last quality, for men in general judge more by the eye than the hand, as all can see but few can feel. Everyone sees what you seem to be, few experience what you really are and these few do not dare to set themselves up against the opinion of the majority supported by the majesty of the state. In the actions of all men and especially princes, where there is no court of appeal, the end is all that counts. Let a prince then concern himself with the acquisition or the
80 maintenance of a state; the means employed will always be considered honorable and praised by all, for the mass of mankind is always swayed by appearances and by the outcome of an enterprise. And in the world there is only the mass, for the few find their place only when the majority has no base of support. A certain prince [1] of our own times, whom it would not be well to name, preaches nothing but peace and faith and yet is the enemy of both, and if he had observed either he would already on numerous occasions have lost both his state and his renown.

# Chapter XIX

## ESSENTIAL TO AVOID BEING HATED OR DESPISED

Now since I have spoken in detail of two of the qualities in my list I shall discuss the rest more briefly and sum up by the general remark that a prince, as I have hinted above, should avoid such things as would make him either hated or despised. If he accomplishes this much he will have done his part and will run no risk from any other infamy he may incur. He will acquire odium, as I have said above, particularly through rapacity and by laying violent hands on the property or the women of his subjects. If the prop-
10 erty and honor of a community be respected, the majority will be content, and only the ambition of a few will be trou-

1. Ferdinand, king of Spain.

blesome, and this may easily be dealt with in various ways. As regards incurring contempt, a prince will be despised if he is considered changeable, frivolous, effeminate, cowardly, or irresolute and he should guard himself against such a reputation as against a most dangerous reef. He should make every effort to give his actions the color of greatness, courage, seriousness, and fortitude. In dealing with his subjects he should see that his judgment is irrevocable and he should acquire such a reputation that no one will dream of deceiving him or trying to get the better of him. A prince acquiring such a reputation is highly thought of, and against one enjoying such respect conspiracy is difficult; it is also difficult to attack him if it is generally understood that he is a man of character and respected by his people.

For a prince must have two concerns: one, internal, regarding his subjects; the other, external, with regard to powerful strangers. From the latter he can defend himself by good arms and good friends—and if his arms are good he will never lack good friends—and internal affairs will give him no trouble so long as foreign affairs are under control, unless they be upset by a conspiracy. Indeed even if foreign affairs should get out of hand, provided his government and manner of living have followed the lines indicated and he does not lose confidence, he will withstand every shock as did the Spartan Nabis.

As for the citizens, even when there is no trouble from outside, one must be on guard against secret conspiracies. A prince may protect himself very well against these by seeing to it that he is neither hated nor despised and by keeping the people satisfied with him, for it is very necessary to win their favor, as I have pointed out at length. One of the most powerful protections that a prince can have against conspiracies is in being neither hated nor despised by the community; for a conspirator always hopes to please the people by the killing of the prince; when, on the other hand, he sees that the people will be hurt rather than pleased, he cannot find the courage to adopt such a course, for any conspiracy is full of infinite difficulties.

We have indeed seen many conspiracies but few successful ones. For a conspirator cannot work alone and he can find no other company save among the malcontents. And as soon as you have revealed yourself to a malcontent you

have furnished him with material to assure his content, for
he has everything to gain by betraying you. And, thus seeing certain advantage on one side and very dubious and
dangerous profit on the other, he will be a rare friend indeed or a most bitter hater of the prince if he keeps faith
60 with you.

And to summarize briefly: on the side of the conspirator
there is nothing but fear, jealousy, and a gnawing anxiety
about the punishment that awaits him, but on his side the
prince has the majesty of the state, the laws, and the protection of his friends as well as of the government, so that
if to all these be added the goodwill of the people it is impossible that anyone will be so rash as to plot against him.
Normally the plotter has much to fear before the accom-
plishment of his evil design but in this case he will have
70 much to fear afterwards from a hostile people and cannot
on this account expect to find comfort anywhere.

Infinite examples could be given, but I will content myself with one from our fathers' generation. Messer Hannibal Bentivogli, grandfather of the present-day Hannibal,
prince of Bologna, was slain by the Canneschi [1] who conspired against him and left only Messer Giovanni, still an
infant; and immediately after the crime the people arose
and slew all the Canneschi. This was simply because of
the devotion of the people of Bologna in those days to the
80 house of the Bentivogli, and indeed it was so strong, that,
as the death of Hannibal left no one able to govern the
state, the Bolognese sent to Florence to seek an individual
who was said to be of Bentivogli blood, though commonly
regarded as the son of a blacksmith, and put the government of the city into his hands until the infant Giovanni
reached an age fit to rule. The conclusion is that when a
prince can count on the goodwill of the people he should
give little heed to conspiracies but when the people are hostile and have only hatred for him he will rightly fear every-
90 thing and everybody. Well governed states and wise
princes have taken every precaution to keep the aristocracy
from becoming embittered and the people satisfied and
content; this is one of the most important concerns of a
prince.

Among the well organized and well governed states of
our day is the Kingdom of France. In that country there

1. In 1445.

are a number of good constitutional measures on which the liberty and the safety of the king depend, the most important of which is Parliament and the authority conferred on it. For the founders of the kingdom, aware of the ambition and arrogance of the nobles, deemed it necessary to put a bit between their teeth, and at the same time, knowing also the hatred based on fear that the community bears against the nobles, sought to give them protection. Yet they did not lay this charge on the king lest he incur the accusation of partiality from one side or the other, but set up instead a third authority that, while laying no burden on the king, might curb the nobles and favor the people. There could hardly be a more prudent nor better measure than this nor one of greater importance to the safety of the king and the kingdom. From this we may make a noteworthy observation that princes should leave the function of distributing charges and burdens to others and preserve for themselves the office of dispensing favors and pardons.

I will repeat my conclusion: a prince must esteem the nobility but never let himself be hated by the people. Reviewing the lives and deaths of many Roman emperors, many might say they were examples proving just the contrary of what I have said, inasmuch as some lived noble lives and showed true greatness of soul and yet lost their empire or were slain by their own people in conspiracy against them. In order to answer this objection I shall analyze the qualities of some of the emperors and shall indicate the causes of their downfalls, which will be found to be in line with what I have said. At the same time I shall call attention to such things as may be worthy of note in the events of those times. I will limit myself to the emperors who came to the purple between Marcus the philosopher and Maximinus: to wit Marcus, Commodus his son, Pertinax, Julian, Severus, his son Antoninus Caracalla, Macrinus, Heliogabalus, Alexander, and Maximinus.

Now the first thing to note is that, whereas other princes have only to contend with the ambition of the aristocracy and the insolence of the people, the Roman emperors had a third problem, which was how to deal with the cruelty and greed of the soldiers. This was the cause of the downfall of many emperors, for it was hard to satisfy both the soldiery and the people, inasmuch as the latter, longing for peace and quiet, prefer a modest prince while the soldiers

140 love a prince of martial spirit, bold, cruel, and rapacious. The Roman soldiers wanted their emperors to practise just such qualities on the people in order to have double pay and to satisfy their own rapacity and cruelty. Thus it came about that the emperors who were unable to acquire either naturally or by skill such prestige as to satisfy either party always came to grief. Most of them, particularly those who came new to the purple, perceiving the problems presented by these two contrary humors, bent their efforts to satisfying the soldiers and thought little of injuring the peo-

150 ple. This was a necessary choice, for when princes must perforce incur hatred from some quarter they will do well to avoid the hatred of the community and when that is not possible at least they should make every effort not to be objectionable to the more powerful groups. Therefore such emperors as had, because of their newness to the purple, need of extraordinary support, would take the side of the soldiers rather than that of the people and this served them well or ill according to their skill in keeping their prestige over their troops. Now Marcus, Pertinax, and Al-

160 exander were all men of modest lives, lovers of justice and enemies of cruelty, humane, and benign, and all of them, for the reasons mentioned above, came to a sorry end, except only Marcus. He lived and died honored by all because he had succeeded to the empire by inheritance and owed nothing either to the soldiers or to the people, and, further, his many virtues, which made him venerated by all, enabled him to keep both these parties in their place, and he was never hated nor despised. But Pertinax was made emperor against the will of the soldiers, who had become

170 used to a licentious life under Commodus and could not tolerate the kind of honest life to which Pertinax wished to lead them. Hence he became odious to them, and thereto was added the contempt that they felt for his advanced years, and so he fell to ruin very shortly after his elevation. Here we may note that hatred may be acquired by good works no less than by bad, and thus, as I pointed out before, a prince wishing to maintain the state is often compelled not to be good. For when the group,—people, soldiery, nobility, whichever it be—on which you see you

180 must depend, is corrupt, you must adapt yourself to its humor and satisfy it and then good works are bad for you.

Now coming to Alexander; here was a man of such

goodness that among other things to his credit it was said of him that in his fourteen years of office no man was sentenced to death by him without a fair trial. Nevertheless, because he was regarded as effeminate and said to be under his mother's guidance, he fell into contempt, and the whole army conspired against him and killed him.

Turning now to the qualities of Commodus, Severus, Antoninus Caracalla, and Maximinus, you will find them just the opposite, for all were extremely rapacious and cruel men. These rulers, desirous of satisfying their troops, did not spare the people any kind of injury that could be inflicted; yet all except Severus came to a bad end. Severus indeed was a man of such character that by keeping his soldiers well disposed to him he was able to reign in peace though he much oppressed the people. For his talents aroused such admiration for him in the people and in the troops that the former were, as it were, amazed and dazzled, and the latter reverent and satisfied. Because the actions of this man as a new prince were great indeed, I should like to show briefly how well he could play both the lion and the fox, both of which natures, as I said before, a prince must know how to imitate. When Severus learned of the incompetence of the emperor Julian, concealing his own ambition, he persuaded his army in Slavonia to march on Rome and avenge the death of Pertinax at the hands of the Imperial Guard, and he was in Rome before it was learned that he had left Slavonia. He was elected emperor by the terrified Senate, and Julian was executed. After this initial success Severus had two obstacles to overcome in making himself master of the state: in Asia, Niger, leader of the armies of Asia, had had himself proclaimed emperor, and, in the West, Albinus too aspired to the purple. Judging it too hazardous to oppose both, Severus decided to attack Niger and deceive Albinus. He therefore wrote the latter that as he had been proclaimed Emperor by the Senate he wished to share the honor with him and he saluted him as Caesar and had him named co-emperor by the Senate. Albinus thought him sincere. But when Severus, having conquered and slain Niger, returned to Rome, he complained to the Senate about Albinus, charging that, unmindful of the benefits conferred on him, his colleague had plotted to kill him, and thus he felt constrained to punish his ingratitude. So he led his army into

France and deprived Albinus of his state and his life. And if we examine attentively the actions of this emperor we shall find in him the ferocious lion and the sly fox and we shall note that he was feared and revered by all and not
230 hated by his armies. Hence it will occasion no surprise that he, though new to the purple, was able to exercise great authority, for his great reputation was his protection against the hatred which his rapacity might have aroused in the people.

His son, Antoninus Caracalla, was a most excellent man too and had such qualities in himself as to make him admired by the people and acceptable to the soldiers, for he was a soldierly man, resistant to all kinds of fatigue and hardship and a scorner of delicate foods or any other kind
240 of softness, and this made him beloved of all his armies. Nonetheless his ferocity and cruelty were so immoderate— for by his infinite executions he did away with the greater part of the population of Rome and all of that of Alexandria—that he became an object of hatred to all and began to be regarded with terror by those who surrounded his person and so was finally slain by a centurion in the midst of his troops. Here we may note that assassinations of this sort that result from the deliberations of men of determined and unshakeable purpose are impossible for
250 a prince to protect himself against, for such a deed may be accomplished by anyone who cares not for his own life. Yet a prince has the less to fear from such deeds as they are in fact very rare. A prince must only take care to inflict no grave injury on any of those whom he employs and who stand near him in the service of the state. This was precisely the error of Antoninus, for he had condemned the brother of the centurion to an ignominious death and threatened the officer himself every day and yet kept him in his bodyguard; this was a policy sure to lead to ruin,
260 as in fact it did.

Commodus, the son of Marcus, came to the throne by hereditary right and would have found it very easy to remain in power, for merely by following the footsteps of his father he would have satisfied both the people and the troops. Yet, being a man of cruel and bestial nature and wishing to practise his rapacity on the people, he curried favor with the army and gave the soldiers free rein, while on the other hand, having no regard for his own dignity,

he descended frequently into the arena to take part in the
gladiatorial combats and committed other acts unworthy 270
of the imperial majesty. Hence he became despicable in the
eyes of the soldiers and, being hated by one party and despised by the other, he was slain, the victim of a conspiracy
formed against him.

We have now to relate the qualities of Maximinus. He
was a man of warlike nature and, as the armies were weary
of the effeminacy of Alexander, whom we have discussed
above, on his death they elected Maximinus to the purple.
He did not, however, wear it long, for two things made
him an object both of hatred and of scorn. One was his 280
humble birth; he had been a shepherd in Thrace and this
was known to all and lowered his dignity in everyone's
eyes; the other his deferred entrance into Rome, which
allowed the reputation of his cruelty to spread abroad
through the harsh and inhuman acts of his prefects in
Rome and other parts of the empire. Thus the whole world
being moved on the one hand by indignation because of
the baseness of his birth and on the other by hatred and
fear of his ferocious cruelty, first Africa, then the Senate
and the people of Rome, and finally all of Italy conspired 290
against him and were joined by his own army. The end
came when his troops, in the difficult siege of Aquileia,
wearied by his cruelty and having scant fear of him on account of his many enemies, turned on him and killed him.

I shall not discuss in detail Heliogabalus nor Macrinus
nor Julian for they were contemptible figures and soon
swept aside, but I shall come now to the conclusion of this
discourse. I will point out that the princes of our time do
not have the problem of satisfying the inordinate demands
of their troops in their states, for, although some considera- 300
tion must be given them, yet this is a matter not difficult to
arrange as none of our princes command armies that are
rooted in the governments and administrations of the provinces, as were the armies of imperial Rome. Thus, if it
was in those days necessary to satisfy the soldiers rather
than the people, this was because the soldiers were more
powerful than the people; nowadays, excepting only the
Turk and the Sultan, princes must satisfy the people, for
they are more powerful than the soldiery. I except the
Turk, as he has about him twelve thousand foot and fif- 310
teen thousand horse on whom the strength and security

of his kingdom depend and he must perforce keep them satisfied beyond any possible consideration for his people. The Kingdom of the Sultan is of the same stamp, for it is entirely at the mercy of the soldiers, whom this monarch, too, must keep friendly at all costs. It is noteworthy that this state of the Sultan is unlike other principalities and similar to the Christian pontificate in that it cannot be called either a hereditary monarchy or a new monarchy, 320 for the new lord and heir to the power is not the son of the previous ruler but one chosen by those who have the authority to make this election. And since the form of government is ancient one cannot describe it as a new state, nor are there found in it any of the difficulties we have enumerated as pertaining to new states. For though the prince be new the laws of the state are old and so set up as to receive him as if he were a hereditary prince.

But to return to our subject. Whoever studies what has been set forth above will see that either hatred or contempt 330 was the ruin of the emperors we have alluded to. And he will understand why each one of them came to his particular end, happy or otherwise, even though some followed one line and others the opposite. For Pertinax and Alexander, as they were new princes, it was idle and dangerous to attempt to imitate Marcus, who inherited the purple; in like manner for Caracalla, Commodus, and Maximinus it was fatal to imitate Severus as they had not sufficient character to follow in his footsteps. So a new prince coming to power in a state cannot imitate the actions of Marcus nor 340 is it essential to imitate those of Severus; rather should he take from Severus such things as may be necessary for the establishment of his authority and from Marcus such things as are proper and productive of renown in maintaining a state already established and secure.

# Chapter XX

## WHETHER THE BUILDING OF FORTRESSES OR OTHER MEASURES TAKEN BY PRINCES ARE USEFUL OR DANGEROUS

Some princes for the security of their state have disarmed their subjects, others have kept subject cities divided in factions; some have encouraged hostility to themselves, others have tried to win over such as were suspect to them in the beginning of their rule; some have built fortresses, others have razed and destroyed them. It is not possible to express an opinion on these actions unless we study a particular state wherein certain measures have to be taken, yet I shall discuss them in such general terms as the material lends itself to. 10

There never was a new prince who disarmed his subjects; on the other hand where they are found unarmed the prince always arms them, for the arms you give your subjects become your own, as those who were suspect become your faithful followers and those who were well disposed to you are encouraged to remain so, and thus all your subjects become your partisans. And since it is impossible to arm all, if those whom you do arm are well treated you can count yourself safe from the others. The distinction in treatment will make the armed ones feel under 20 obligation to you, and the others will forgive you, deeming it natural that those who have greater obligations and must face greater dangers should also have greater merit in your eyes. If, however, you disarm your people, you begin by offending all of them, showing that you do not trust them either through fear or lack of confidence, and the suspicion of either will arouse hatred against you. Further, as you cannot well remain without any arms, you will have to turn to mercenaries, whose character we have examined above, and even if they were good they could not be strong 30 enough to protect you against powerful enemies and doubtful citizens.

Hence, as I have said, a new prince in a new state has always set up measures for arming the citizens. History is full of examples of this. However, when a prince acquires a new state that is added to his old possessions, then it is necessary to disarm everyone in the new state save only those who have already declared for him. Even these must, gradually and as opportunity permits, be made weak and
40 ineffective, and it must be so ordered that all the arms of the state are in the hands of your own men who come from your hereditary state.

Those who were accounted wise among our ancestors used to say that Pistoia had to be held by factions and Pisa by fortresses, and following this rule they encouraged factionalism in some of their subject cities, in order the more easily to keep their grip on them. In times when there was a certain balance of power in Italy, this policy was good, but I hardly think one could offer it as a precept for
50 today, for I do not think that division fomented among the people is useful to anyone; indeed on the approach of an enemy a divided city must necessarily fall, for the weaker party will always join forces with the invader and overcome the other faction. The Venetians, following, I believe, the policy alluded to, always fostered the Guelf and Ghibelline parties in their subject cities and, while they never allowed open feuds to break out, they nonetheless encouraged partisan feelings so that the citizens would be absorbed in their own differences and would not turn on
60 their masters. In the sequel, however, this policy was seen as certainly not working to their advantage for when the Venetian forces were broken at Vailà one party of the subject cities took courage and deprived the Venetians of their whole state. Such tactics further indicate a weakness in the prince, for in a vigorous state divisions of this nature will never be tolerated, as they are useful in times of peace when they allow the citizens to be more easily managed, but when war comes their weakness becomes immediately apparent.

70 Beyond doubt the greatness of princes lies in their ability to overcome obstacles and opposition, and therefore fortune, especially when she is moved to magnify a new prince, who has more need of acquiring fame than an established ruler, creates enemies for him and obliges him to take action against them in order that he may cast them

down and climb, as it were, even higher on the ladder his
enemies have provided. On this account many hold that
a new prince, if he has the chance, should cleverly encourage some enmity so that by overcoming it his glory will
shine the brighter.

Princes, and especially new ones, have found the men
whom they regarded with mistrust in the beginning of
their rule more trustworthy and more useful than those
whom they had confidence in at the start. Pandolfo Petrucci,[1] Prince of Siena, governed his state with the help of
those he held suspect rather than the others. One cannot discuss this matter in general terms, for circumstances differ in
different cases. I shall, however, say this much: if those who
are hostile in the early period of setting up the new state are
in such a position as to need support to maintain themselves, they can always be won over easily by the prince,
and are the more obliged to serve him loyally as they know
that their services must cancel out his earlier mistrust of
them. Thus the prince will find such men more useful than
those who, having always served him with confidence, may
be careless about his affairs. And since it is related to the
subject here, I will suggest that a prince who has acquired
a new state with the aid of those dwelling within it should
consider carefully what motives caused his allies to take
his part. And if it was not natural devotion to him, but,
rather, discontent with the previous government, then he
will find it painful and difficult to keep on friendly terms
with them, for they will be impossible to satisfy. Examining
this matter well and bearing in mind examples in ancient
and modern history, we shall see that it is always easier to
make friends of those who were content in the old government and hence initially enemies of the new prince than to
keep on good terms with those who favored his occupation
because they were discontented with the former regime.

It has been the custom of princes desirous of keeping
their hold on their states to erect fortresses as a check
against any who might wish to rise against them and to
have a secure refuge against the first shock. I am disposed
to approve of this usage, which has been sanctioned by
time. Nonetheless in our day we have seen Messer Niccolò
Vitelli dismantle two fortresses in Città di Castello in order

1. 1452-1512; ruled Siena from 1497 to his death.

to retain possession of that state. Guid'Ubaldo, Duke of Urbino, on his return after being driven out by Cesare Borgia, had all the forts in that province razed to the ground and considered himself much less likely to lose his state a second time. The Bentivogli followed a similar course when they returned to Bologna. Fortresses may then be useful or not according to circumstances, and as in one way they are useful in another they may be harmful. We may sum up this matter thus: a prince who has more to fear from his own people than from foreigners, should build forts, and one who has more to fear from the foreigner should not build them. The Castle built in Milan by Francesco Sforza has been and will yet be the cause of more woe to his house than any other disorder in that state. The best fortress a prince can have is simply in not being hated by his people, for if the people hate you your fortresses will not save you, inasmuch as your people, once in arms, will easily find foreigners to take their part. In our times the only case we have seen in which a fortress has been useful to a ruler was that of the Countess of Forlì [2] after the death of her husband Girolamo. In that case the fortress permitted her to escape the fury of the people and await the help from Milan which enabled her to win back her state. For at that time circumstances were such that the people could count on no foreign aid. Yet fortifications were of little avail to this same countess on the later occasion when she was attacked by Cesare Borgia and her people joined the attacking forces. So for her too, both on the first occasion and the second, it would have been safer to have the goodwill of the people rather than fortifications. So I will approve of those who build forfortresses and of those who do not, according to the circumstances, but I shall criticize any who, trusting in them, hold the hatred of the people to be of little account.

2. Caterina Sforza (1463-1509). In 1488 her husband, Girolamo Riario, was murdered, and the people of Forlì rose against her. The attack by Cesare Borgia came in 1499.

# Chapter XXI

## HOW A PRINCE SHOULD CONDUCT HIMSELF IN ORDER TO ACQUIRE PRESTIGE

Nothing brings a prince into greater respect than the undertaking of great enterprises and setting a glorious example. In our day we have Ferdinand of Aragon, the present King of Spain. He may almost be called a new prince for, from being a very weak king, he has risen in fame and glory to be the leading monarch in Christendom. If his actions be studied, they will all be found great and some of them really extraordinary. Shortly after ascending to the throne, he attacked Granada, and that undertaking was the foundation of his state. For first of all he carried on the siege at his leisure and without fear of interference, and he kept the attention of the barons of Castille fixed on this war and thus unlikely to consider changes in the state, so that, almost without their being aware of it, he acquired great prestige and authority over them. The money from the Church and from the people enabled him to pay the troops and, in the course of that long war, to lay the foundations for his own army, which has since won so much honor for him. Furthermore, in order to prepare for greater enterprises, and always making use of the pretext of religion, he adopted the piously cruel policy of driving the Moors from his kingdom and despoiling them; herein his conduct could not have been more admirable and extraordinary. Still with the same pretext he attacked Africa, made the campaign in Italy, and has recently turned on the French. Thus he has continually been weaving some great design, which has arrested and amazed the minds of his subjects and kept them absorbed in the development of his plans. His projects have arisen naturally one out of the other and thus have afforded no time for men to pause and organize against him.

A prince should also give a good example in the matter of internal government, as in the case of Messer Bernabò

of Milan,[1] rewarding or punishing, as the occasion arises,
the citizens who do good or evil in the service of the state,
but taking care that the rewards or punishments be such
as to cause comment. Above all a prince should see to it
that his every action may add to his fame of greatness or
excellence.

40    A prince is also esteemed when he shows himself a true
friend or a true enemy, that is, when, without reservation,
he takes his stand with one side or the other. This is always
wiser than trying to be neutral, for if two powerful neighbors of yours fall out they are either of such sort that the
victor may give you reason to fear him or they are not.
In either case it will be better for you to take sides and
wage an honest war. In the first case, if you do not show
your sympathies, you will be an easy prey for the winner
to the delight and satisfaction of the loser, and you will
50    have no reason to expect anyone to defend you or give you
refuge. For the winner will not care for unreliable friends
who may abandon him in adversity, and the loser will not
welcome you since you were not willing to take up arms
and share the hazards of his fortune.

When Antiochus, invited by the Aetolians, had passed
over into Greece to drive out the Romans, he sent spokes-
men to the Achaeans, who were the allies of the Romans,
urging them to keep out of the war. The Romans on their
part were urging the Achaeans to join them. The situation
60    was discussed before the Council of the Achaeans, and
when the legate of Antiochus attempted to persuade them
to remain neutral, the Roman envoy replied: "As to the
statement that it is best and most profitable to your state to
take no part in our war, nothing is further from the truth,
for if you do not come into it you will be the prize of the
victors without any prestige left to you and with no hope
of consideration." And it will always fall out that a party
unfriendly to you will ask you to remain neutral and those
who are friendly will ask you to join them in the war.
70    Irresolute princes, in order to avoid present dangers, usually
follow the path of neutrality and more often than not are
ruined. But if the prince chooses his side boldly, and his
ally wins, even though the latter be powerful and the prince
at his mercy, nonetheless there is a bond of obligation and

1. Bernabò Visconti (1323-1385).

friendship, and mankind is never so faithless as to show ingratitude under such circumstances by turning on friends. Besides, victories are never so complete that the victor need have no caution or respect for justice. But if your ally be the loser then he will welcome you and, as long as he can, he will give you aid and thus you will have a companion 80 in your ill fortune which may yet rise again.

As for the second case, when the two contestants are of such stature that you will have nothing to fear from the victor, it is even more prudent to take part in the war for you will accomplish the ruin of one with the aid of the other who, had he been wise, should rather have supported him. For with your aid he is sure to win and, winning, to put himself in your power. And here it may be noted that a prince should never ally himself with one more powerful to attack another unless absolutely driven by necessity, as 90 in the abovementioned cases. For if your powerful ally wins, you are at his mercy, and princes should avoid as much as possible being at the mercy of another. The Venetians joined France against the Duke of Milan when they could well have dispensed with their ally, and from this alliance came their ruin.[2] Yet there are times when there is no help for it, as in the case of the Florentines when the Pope and the Spanish sent their armies to attack Lombardy,[3] and then a prince must join one of the parties for the reasons set forth in the preceding paragraphs. 100

Let no state think that it can always adopt a safe course; rather should it be understood that all choices involve risks, for the order of things is such that one never escapes one danger without incurring another; prudence lies in weighing the disadvantages of each choice and taking the least bad as good.

A prince too must always show himself a lover of virtue and quick to honor those who excel in the various arts. Furthermore, he should encourage his citizens and enable them to go about their affairs in tranquility whether in 110 commerce, agriculture, or any other kind of activity, so that one man may not refrain from improving his possessions for fear lest they be taken from him, nor another hesitate to engage in commerce for fear of taxes. Rather should a prince reward such citizens and any others who

2. See Chapter III.
3. In 1512.

may in any way enrich his state or his city. He should also, on the appropriate occasions, offer festivals and spectacles for the diversion of his people, and, since every city is divided into guilds or clans, he should be mindful of these groups and occasionally mingle with them, giving an example of his humanity and munificence, always preserving, however, the majesty of his dignity, for this should never be allowed to suffer in any way.

# Chapter XXII

## THE PRINCE'S MINISTERS

The choice of his ministers is of no slight importance to a prince, and their qualities will vary according to the wisdom of the prince. The first opinion to be formed of a prince and his intelligence will depend on the men we see around him. When these are able and loyal, we can be sure that the prince is a wise man, for he has known how to recognize their ability and keep them loyal. If they are not of this nature, then we are entitled to form a poor opinion of the prince, for in this choice of ministers he has made a primary mistake.

No one who knew Antonio da Venafro, the minister of Pandolfo Petrucci, Prince of Siena, could fail to judge this prince to be a most intelligent man simply on the evidence of his choice of a minister. There are indeed three kinds of minds: one understands things by itself, the second can understand what is explained to it by others, and the third cannot understand either directly or by the demonstration of others. The first kind is most excellent, the second is good, and the third is useless. Pandolfo, if not of the first rank of mentality, must clearly have been of the second, for if a prince has sufficient judgment to distinguish between good and bad words or deeds, even if he does not have any initiative himself, he can distinguish between the bad and good works of his minister and thus correct the former and praise the latter. A minister cannot hope to deceive a master of this sort and so keeps on the right track.

As to how a prince may determine the quality of a min-

ister, there is this method which never fails. When you see
the minister thinking more of himself than of you, and
seeking his own advantage in all his actions, you may be 30
sure that he will never make a good minister, nor can you
ever trust him. For a man to whom is entrusted the charge
of the state must never think of himself but always of the
prince and he must concern himself only with his master's
affairs. On his part, to insure loyalty, the prince must take
care of his minister, bestowing honors and riches on him,
and put him under obligation by sharing distinctions and
offices with him. The honors and the riches thus showered
on him will prevent him from seeking the like from another source, and the offices allotted to him will make him 40
afraid of change or revolution since his eminence depends
on the prince. When the master and minister are of this
nature, then they may have the greatest confidence in each
other, otherwise either one or the other will come to a
bad end.

# Chapter XXIII

## HOW TO AVOID FLATTERERS

I do not wish to omit a most important consideration
concerning a pitfall very difficult for princes to avoid unless
they be most prudent men and wise in their choice of ministers. I refer to flatterers, who abound in all courts. Men
are so complacent about their own affairs and so easily deceived in matters touching them that this pestilence of
adulation is very hard to guard against and, in attempting
to defend oneself against it, one may run the risk of becoming despicable. This comes about because there is only
one way to guard against flattery and that is by letting it 10
be understood that you will not be offended by plain
speaking; yet if everyone may speak boldly to you, you will
suffer loss of respect. A wise prince therefore should try
to follow a third course, choosing men of wisdom as officials of his state and to these alone conceding the right to
speak freely. They should be allowed to speak frankly only
when they are consulted by the prince, but he on the other

hand should consult them on all matters and listen to their views and then make up his own mind after due considera-
20 tion. In his councils with them and with each minister individually, he should make it clear that frank and honest advice is welcome. But except for his trusted ministers he should refuse to listen to anyone and once his mind is made up he should stick to his decision and follow through. One who does otherwise will either come to grief through flatterers or vacillate between the different opinions and hence suffer in general esteem.

On this subject I should like to give a modern example. Pre' Luca, a servant of Maximilian,[1] the present Emperor,
30 said, speaking of his master, that he never consulted with anyone and yet never carried out anything in his own way. This comes of following a line of conduct directly contrary to the one suggested above. For the Emperor, being a secretive man, does not discuss his plans with anyone and asks no man's advice; then, when his projects are put into effect and begin to be clear to all, they are opposed by his ministers, and the Emperor, not being firm of purpose, abandons his policy. Hence it is that his decisions of today are rejected tomorrow and it is impossible to know what
40 he is planning to do and no confidence can be placed in his decisions.

A prince then should always listen to advice but only when he asks for it and not when others suggest it, and he should discourage his advisors from speaking unless asked, yet he should ask frequently and listen patiently, indeed, he should be concerned if he suspects that some one, out of respect, is not telling him the plain truth. And if some think that certain princes who have the reputation of prudence are not so by nature but only because of the
50 good advice of their counsellors, they are making a great mistake. For this general rule is infallible; a prince who is without any wisdom himself, cannot be well advised. The only exception would be a prince who would put himself entirely in the hands of a wise minister, and in that case his government would be good but would be of short duration, for his minister would soon deprive him of his state. But a prince who consults with more than one advisor, unless he be a wise man, will never know how to

1. Maximilian I (1459-1519). Traditional imperial pretensions and his marriage to Bianca Sforza made him active in Italian politics.

coordinate the advice given him. For each of his advisors
will see the matter from his own point of view, and a stupid 60
prince will be unable to make allowances and distinctions.
Advisors are of necessity of such a nature because unless
men are compelled to be good they will invariably turn out
bad. And in conclusion we may say that the prudence of
the prince does not come from the advice given him but, to
the contrary, good advice whatever be its immediate source,
has its true origin in the wisdom of the prince.

# Chapter XXIV

## WHY THE PRINCES OF ITALY HAVE LOST
## THEIR STATES

The suggestions made above, if acted upon, will make a
new prince seem one well established and will set him up
more firmly and securely in his state than if he had had
it for years. For the actions of a new prince are much more
closely scrutinized than those of an established one, and
when they are seen to be intelligent and effective they may
win over more men and create stronger bonds of obligation
than have been felt to the old line, inasmuch as the minds
of men are wrapped up in the present and not in the past
and when they find their advantage in the present they 10
enjoy it and do not look back. Indeed they will undertake
to defend him if the prince gives proper attention to his
part. So he will have increased glory from having set up a
new state and enriched and strengthened it with good
arms, good laws, good alliances, and good examples, even
as greater disgrace will be the lot of one born a prince who
has lost his state through folly.

If we consider the lords of Italy that have lost their states
in our day, such as the King of Naples, the Duke of Milan
and others, we shall find they all made one common mis- 20
take in the matter of arms which we have discussed at
length above, and that, furthermore, some of them have
aroused the hostility of the people, and others who had the
the favor of the people were not able to protect themselves
against the nobles. For it is only these defects that can

cause the loss of a state having sufficient resources to put an army in the field. Philip of Macedon—not the father of Alexander, but the one defeated by Titus Quinctius—ruled over a state that was very small in comparison to the Roman possessions and to Greece that joined in attacking him; nevertheless because he was skilled in military affairs and knew both how to win the favor of the people and assure the cooperation of the nobles he was able to stand up under a long war against these powerful foes, and though in the end he lost a few cities yet he preserved his kingdom. So these princes of ours who had been for many years entrenched in their states have no cause to complain of fortune because they have lost them; the fault lies rather in their own ineptitude, for, as in tranquil times they had given no thought to the possibility of change (a common failing of men, who rarely think of storms to come while the sun yet shines), adversity caught them unprepared and their first thought was of flight and not defense, hoping that their people would weary of the insolence of the conqueror and so recall them. This is a good resource, to be sure, when there is no other, but it is ill to neglect other remedies in favor of such a hope, for certainly we should never be willing to fall simply in the belief that some one will pick us up again. For this may not happen, and if it does happen it does not help in your salvation, for it is a cowardly kind of defense and not based on your own efforts, and the only good, reliable, and enduring defense is one that comes from yourself and your own valor and ability.

# Chapter XXV

## THE INFLUENCE OF FORTUNE ON HUMAN AFFAIRS AND HOW IT MAY BE COUNTERED

I am not ignorant of the fact that many have held and hold the opinion that the things of this world are so ordered by fortune and God that the prudence of mankind may effect little change in them, indeed is of no avail at all. On this basis it could be argued that there is no point

in making any effort, but we should rather abandon our-
selves to destiny. This opinion has been the more widely
held in our day on account of the great variations in things
that we have seen and are still witnessing and which are
entirely beyond human conjecture. Sometimes indeed,  10
thinking on such matters, I am minded to share that
opinion myself. Nevertheless I believe, if we are to keep
our free will, that it may be true that fortune controls half
of our actions indeed but allows us the direction of the
other half, or almost half. I would compare fortune to a
river in flood, which when it breaks its bonds, deluges the
surrounding plains, tears up trees and dwellings, here
washing away the land and there building up new de-
posits. All flee before it, everyone must bow before the fury
of the flood, for there is no checking it. Yet though this be  20
so it does not signify that in quiet times men cannot make
some provision against it, building levees and dikes so that
when the river rises it may follow a channel prepared for it
or at least have its first onrush rendered less impetuous and
harmful. In like fashion fortune displays her greatest effect
where there is no organized ability to resist and hence she
directs her bolts where there have been no defenses or bul-
warks prepared against her. And if you will consider Italy,
the scene of the variations we have mentioned above and
the motivating center thereof, you will find it an open field  30
without dikes and without any kind of protection. Had it
been protected by proper valor and ability, as were Germany, France, and Spain, it would not have suffered such
great changes from the flood, which indeed might never
have come. This I think should suffice as an argument
against fortune in general.

Coming now to particular cases, I will note how we see
such a prince reign happily today and meet his downfall
tomorrow without any visible change in his nature and
character. This is a result of causes we have already dis-  40
cussed, and a prince who depends entirely on fortune will
not prosper when fortune changes. I further believe that a
prince is fortunate when his conduct is in accord with the
times and unsuccessful if his behavior is not so in tune. For
we observe of men as they follow out the course of action
necessary to the ends they seek, whether glory or riches,
that one works cautiously, another impetuously, or one
uses violence and another astuteness, or one is patient and

another the contrary, yet success may attend any of these
50 methods. And we may see that of two of the cautious type
one attains his ends where the other fails, and similarly
we may see two succeed though using different methods,
one deliberate and the other impetuous, and this all depends on the temper of the times and whether or not it be
in accord with the method of procedure. Hence it comes
about, as I have said, that two using different methods may
come to the same end, and of two following the same
method one may succeed and the other fail. Herein lies the
variation in prosperity, for if one prince conducts himself
60 with patience and caution and the times are right for such
conduct he will prosper, but if times and circumstances
change and he does not alter his behavior he will fall. Nor
is there any man so wise as to be able to adapt himself to
such changes, both because we cannot be other than as
nature inclines us and because one who has prospered by
following one kind of policy will not be persuaded to abandon it. Hence the cautious man, when the time comes for
bold action, is incapable of it and so falls, for if nature could
be changed with the variation of times and circumstances
70 fortune would not change.

Julius II proceeded boldly in every action, and the times
and conditions were so favorable to this style of behavior
that his affairs always turned out well. Consider his first
undertaking against Bologna in the lifetime of Messer Giovanni Bentivogli. The Venetians were not pleased, nor the
Spanish; the French were still discussing this enterprise,
nevertheless Julius with his characteristic boldness and
dash directed the expedition in person. This move gave
pause to the Venetians and the Spanish: the former were
80 frightened and the latter saw an opportunity to recover the
Kingdom of Naples. Further, his action carried along the
King of France, for when the latter, anxious for the Pope's
friendship in order to crush the Venetians, saw that Julius
had acted he concluded he could not refuse to supply him
with troops without openly offending him. So with his
bold move Julius was able to carry out what no other Pontiff following normal human prudence would have accomplished, for had he decided not to leave Rome until all
terms were clear and everything in order, as any other Pope
90 would have done, he would never have been successful.
The King of France would have had a thousand excuses,

and the others would have made a thousand threats. I shall not speak of his other actions, for they were all of the same nature and all crowned with success. The brevity of his life afforded him no opportunity to experience the contrary effect, yet if he had ever come upon times requiring the use of caution his downfall would have been certain, for he could never have deviated from the character with which nature endowed him.

My conclusion is, then, that, as fortune is variable and men fixed in their ways, men will prosper so long as they are in tune with the times and will fail when they are not. However, I will say that in my opinion it is better to be bold than cautious, for fortune is a woman and whoever wishes to win her must importune and beat her, and we may observe that she is more frequently won by this sort than by those who proceed more deliberately. Like a woman, too, she is well disposed to young men, for they are less circumspect and more violent and more bold to command her.

# Chapter XXVI

## EXHORTATION TO FREE ITALY FROM THE BARBARIANS

Reflecting on the matters set forth above and considering within myself whether the times were propitious in Italy at present to honor a new prince and whether there is at hand the matter suitable for a prudent and virtuous leader to mold in a new form, giving honor to himself and benefit to the citizens of the country, I have arrived at the opinion that all circumstances now favor such a prince, and I cannot think of a time more propitious for him than the present. If, as I said, it was necessary in order to make apparent the virtue of Moses, that the people of Israel should be enslaved in Egypt, and that the Persians should be oppressed by the Medes to provide an opportunity to illustrate the greatness and the spirit of Cyrus, and that the Athenians should be scattered in order to show the excellence of Theseus, thus at the present time, in order to reveal the valor of an Italian spirit it was essential that Italy

should fall to her present low estate, more enslaved than
the Hebrews, more servile than the Persians, more disunited than the Athenians, leaderless and lawless, beaten,
20 despoiled, lacerated, overrun and crushed under every kind
of misfortune. And although before now we have seen
some slight thread of hope in a certain individual such as
to make us believe him sent for our redemption, yet we
have seen him, too, unhappily betrayed by fortune at the
very zenith of his career.[1] So Italy now, left almost lifeless,
awaits the coming of one who will heal her wounds, putting an end to the sacking and looting in Lombardy and
the spoliation and extortions in the Realm of Naples and
Tuscany, and cleanse her sores that have been so long fes-
30 tering. Behold how she prays God to send her some one to
redeem her from the cruelty and insolence of the barbari-
ans. See how she is ready and willing to follow any banner
so long as there be some one to take it up. Nor has she at
present any hope of finding her redeemer save only in your
illustrious house[2] which has been so highly exalted both
by its own merits and by fortune and which has been favored by God and the Church, of which it is now ruler.

This task will not be too difficult for you, if you bear in
mind the actions and the lives of the heroes mentioned
40 above. For although they were extraordinary and wonder-
ful men yet they were still men and each one had a less favorable opportunity than the present affords, for their
undertaking was no more just than this nor more easy, nor
was God any more friendly to them. In this case there is
great justice for that war is just which is necessary and
arms are merciful when there is no hope save in them.
Here the ground is ready, and where the ground is prepared there cannot be great difficulties provided that the
measures of the models I have cited be adopted. Further-
50 more, here we have seen unparalleled signs from God, the
seas have divided, a cloud has shown the way, water has
poured from the stone, here the manna has fallen, all
things have conspired for your greatness; the rest you must
now do yourselves. God does not want to do everything for
us, so as not to deprive us of free will nor take from us that
portion of glory which is ours.

Nor is it a matter for surprise if none of the other Italian
leaders I have named has been able to accomplish what we

1. Probably a reference to Cesare Borgia.　　2. The Medici.

hope of your house, nor if, in so many revolutions in Italy
and so many military operations, it may appear that the  60
martial virtue of the country is dead. This is simply because the old methods of warfare were not good and there
has been no one to teach new methods. Nothing sheds so
much honor on a man newly come to power as new laws
and new methods discovered by him. When these things
are well founded and have some element of greatness in
them, they make him revered and admired, and in Italy
the matter is not lacking to receive the impress of such
new forms. In this country there is great virtue in the limbs
if only it can be found in the head. Think of the duels and  70
the meetings of small groups, and remember how the Italians are always superior, in strength, in dexterity, and in
wit. But when we look at armies they do not come into the
discussion and this is because of the weakness of the leaders. Those of them who know their trade are disobedient,
and each man thinks he knows best, nor has there been
yet any general so preeminent either in fortune or talent
as to make the others yield. Hence it is that throughout
this period, in all the wars of the last twenty years, a wholly
Italian army has always given a poor account of itself, for  80
example, at the Taro, Alessandria, Capua, Genoa, Vailà,
Bologna, and Mestri.[3] If your illustrious house then will
be pleased to imitate these great men who were the re-
deemers of their countries, it is first of all neecssary, as an
absolute essential to the undertaking, that it provide itself with troops of its own, for one cannot have more
faithful, reliable, nor effective troops than these. And
though each of them will be good yet they will be even better when they see themselves led by a prince of their own
and honored and cared for by him. Hence it is necessary to  90
build up such an army and thus to be ready to defend the
country with Italian valor against foreigners. And though
the Swiss and the Spanish infantry are accounted formidable yet both have their shortcomings, and a third kind

3. Il Taro is better known as the battle of Fornovo (1495) in
which the army of Charles VIII outwitted the Italian confederation
trying to intercept him on his return to France. Alessandria (1499),
Capua (1501), Genoa (1507), Bologna (1511), were taken by
French troops in various campaigns in Italy. Mestri was burnt by
troops of the Holy League (Imperial, Papal, Milanese and Spanish)
as they moved to attack the Venetians, whom they defeated in the
ensuing battle at Vicenza (1513).

might therefore not only take the field against them but even confidently expect to beat them. For the Spanish cannot withstand cavalry, and the Swiss may be expected to fear infantry if they meet them in the field of such stubbornness as they are themselves. Thus we have seen and experience will show that the Spanish are unable to withstand the French cavalry and the Swiss may be broken by Spanish infantry. And although we have not had a fair test of the latter statement yet we had a sample at Ravenna.[4] Here the Spanish were opposed to the Germans, whose order was similar to the Swiss, and the agile Spaniards, with the aid of their spiked shields, got under the pikes of the Germans and attacked them with impunity while the Germans were helpless to defend themselves, and had it not been for the cavalry charging them the Spaniards would have annihilated them all.

Hence, as we are aware of the defects of these two sorts of infantry, it will be possible to set up a new kind, firm against horse and not afraid of infantry. This can be done, not through a new kind of weapon, but rather a new formation. This is the sort of innovation that will shed luster on a new prince. This opportunity, therefore, should not be allowed to pass, and Italy, after such a long wait, must be allowed to behold her redeemer. I cannot describe the joy with which he will be received in all these provinces which have suffered so much from the foreign deluge, nor with what thirst for vengeance, nor with what firm devotion, what solemn delight, what tears! What gates could be closed to him, what people could deny him obedience, what envy could withstand him, what Italian could withhold allegiance from him? THIS BARBARIAN OCCUPATION STINKS IN THE NOSTRILS OF ALL OF US. Let your illustrious house then take up this cause with the spirit and the hope with which one undertakes a truly just enterprise so that under the banner of your house the country may be ennobled and under its auspices the verses of Petrarch may come true:

> Then Roman valor shall the foe engage,
> And win swift triumph o'er barbarian rage;
> For martial virtue, our forefathers' pride,
> In true Italian hearts has never died.

1. See Introduction.

# Bibliography

The reader wishing to know more about Machiavelli and his times will find the following books easily available and informative.

Burckhardt, Jacob, *The Civilization of the Renaissance in Italy.*
Gilbert, Allan H., *Machiavelli, The Prince And Other Works.*
Merejkowski, Dmitri, *The Romance of Leonardo da Vinci.*
Prezzolini, *Niccolò Machiavelli the Florentine.*
Roeder, Ralph, *The Man of the Renaissance.*
Sabatini, Raphael, *The Life of Cesare Borgia.*
Sforza, Carlo, *The Living Thoughts of Machiavelli.*
Symonds, J. A., *The Age of the Despots.*
Villari, Pasquale, *Niccolò Machiavelli and His Times.*
Young, G. F., *The Medici.*

## NOTE

The edition of the Italian text of *The Prince* generally regarded as definitive may be found in *Niccolò Machiavelli, Tutte le Opere, a cura di Guido Mazzoni e Mario Casella,* Florence, 1929. For some passages however the present translation follows the edition of *L. A. Burd,* Oxford, 1891.

# INDEX OF PROPER NAMES IN
# TEXT AND NOTES